VANISHING FRANCE

Photographs by Harold Chapman

John L. Hess **VANISHING FRANCE**

NYT *Quadrangle / The New York Times Book Co.*

Library of Congress Cataloging in Publication Data

Hess, John L
   Vanishing France.

   1. France—Civilization—1901-   I. Chapman,
Harold, ill.   II. Title.
DC412.H47   944.08   74-77944
ISBN 0-8129-0483-4

Design: Charles Kaplan

To Karen

CONTENTS

INTRODUCTION

At once urbane and earthy, civilized and sensual, la Doulce France has seduced the foreigner ever since Caesar subdued the stubborn Gaul. The Romans came and saw and were finally conquered. The Moors and Vikings, too, and the Germans, who still say, "as happy as God in France." And the Americans, led by Ben Franklin, who instantly recognized France as Everyman's second patrie.

My own seduction came at middle age, when at the end of 1963 I was sent to Paris by *The New York Times* on a temporary assignment that I stretched to nearly a decade. It was the best of times. The tragedy of the Occupation was buried in the French subconscious, and the nation had finally emerged from the folly of colonial wars. She was free to pursue Progress and Prosperity; to become, in short, more like America.

My new mistress was changing before my eyes. A century earlier, a French minister had told a delegation protesting the property qualification for voting, "Enrichissez-vous, messieurs." Now, a Minister of Development—a building promoter by trade—could sneer to other protesters, "I am not a fanatic about green spaces." Chateaux and their parks gave way to suburban developments, town mansions yielded to nondescript high-rises, shaded village squares became parking lots, and concrete condominiums overwhelmed the fishing ports and penetrated the solitudes of the Alps. Thousands of kilometers of trees were felled to widen roads and speed the newly motorized Frenchmen to their crowded new resorts. Old cafés were transformed into synthetic "pubs" and "drugstores," and commercials were introduced on television to promote deodorants, processed cheese, industrial poultry, dehydrated mashed potatoes, and packaged bread. The narrow streets where only recently, as Simenon recalls, every season had its own fragrance, were now filled year-round with automobile fumes, to such a point that huge vacuum cleaners were installed in a desperate experiment to clear the air. Yet most of the cobbled walk on the Right Bank of the Seine, where men fished for gudgeon under the great chestnut trees, was destroyed to make way for an expressway, and a matching road was planned for the Left Bank. In every direction, the great vistas of Paris are now despoiled by skyscrapers, topped by the hideous Tour Montparnasse.

This largest of office buildings in Europe was sponsored by Americans, as was the World Trade Center in New York, which replaced our own Halles, the old Washington Street Market. But if American promoters were active in transforming France, other Americans were among those who cried a warning. We had been through it before, and could testify to the damage that unbridled enterprise would inflict on what we now call the quality of life.

As often as the routine chores of journalism would permit, I hastened to record in print the personality of a France that was disappearing. Occasionally, a dispatch to *The New York Times*, picked up by the Parisian press, may have helped to avert a folly: the hecatomb of trees along the highways was restricted, the landmark Palais d'Orsay beside the Seine was saved from promoters who wanted to replace it with a Hilton-style hotel, and Marcel Dassault announced in an

IX

interview with me that he had abandoned his project to replace the handsome structures on the Rond-Point des Champs-Elysées with a pair of office buildings.

The victories were few, however. More often, I had to report defeats, as in the obituary of Les Halles that opens this collection. I should note that as far as possible all these pieces appear here as they were written, before encountering the slings and arrows of daily editing. (A few were not published at all.) I should add that in spite of the elegiac note, these were happy years, all told, and if much damage was done, much charm remains, and Frenchmen are more determined than ever before to preserve their heritage.

Vive la France.

X

Part One **LE PROGRES**

THE END OF LES HALLES

Paris—February, 1969

Eight centuries of colorful and turbulent history are drawing to a close as Les Halles departs from the medieval heart of Paris.

What Emile Zola called "the belly of Paris," a food market that was also the roaring center of the city's life and the cherished resort of travelers and Parisians, is being transplanted to an ultramodern rectangular complex of sheds near Orly, ten miles to the south. Forty fleets of trucks —the vehicles that doomed Les Halles by creating a 24-hour traffic jam there—began the operation under direction of a staff of military logistics officers. First went the flower merchants, taking the color with them from the teeming streets to their new air-conditioned shed. Then it was the B.O.F. (beurre, oeufs, fromage, or butter, eggs, and cheese), then the fruit and vegetables, finally the fish.

Behind them they leave a bereft community of retailers and bistrot keepers. "My heart is heavy," said Annie Doy, a white-haired librarian. "Every morning this week, I have walked to work the long way, to see it again, because it hurts."

Its history is written in street names. Rue des Petit Champs—street of the Little Fields, in Roman times called Campelli, then Champeaux, where Louis VI, better known as Louis the Fat, founded Les Halles in 1135, before Notre Dame was built. Rue des Poissonnières, where the fish came down from the north coast. Rues au Lard (pork), de la Cossonnerie (game and poultry), de la Boucherie (meat), Quai de la Mégisserie (hides), Lavandière (lavender). Other trades that once shared the market have left their mark in the rues des Orfevres (silversmiths), de la Coutellerie (cutlery), Lingerie and Ferronerie (ironware). It was in Ferronerie that Henry IV, his carriage caught in a traffic jam, was assassinated in 1610.

The grimmer aspects of life in Les Halles are also commemorated in the streets called La Grand Truanderie (big racketeering) whose opposite side is La Petite Truanderie, Vide-Gousset (purse-snatcher), and Brise Miche (breakleg). Citizens were commended rather to take the Rue des Bons Enfants. Else they might end on the Rue de l'Arbre Sec (the dry tree—i.e., the gibbet) or La Pirouette. This tiny street, the length of one narrow housefront, commemorates the revolving pillory where merchants who gave short weight were locked head and foot and slowly rotated as they were pelted by the mob. In one of the many uprisings that began in Les Halles, La Pirouette was burned down, and the executioner with it, in 1516. Rebuilt, it was finally razed during the Revolution.

A few steps away is St. Eustache, the great Gothic church where Louis XIV made his first communion, and where Molière, son of a Halles merchant, had his baptism and his funeral. As Paris grew, Les Halles spread, covering the mass graveyard now marked by the famous Fontaine des Innocents. In 1854, the architect Victor Baltard built ten vast iron pavilions that then comprised the most modern food depot in the world. Soon, however, the market overflowed into the streets around it, and among the mountains of produce arose a hive of tiny satellite businesses: the knife sharpeners, the barrowmen, the collectors of scraps, the sellers of wine, fried

2

potatoes, and sausages. As the major work of the market began around midnight, Paris revelers developed the tradition of greeting the dawn at Les Halles, eating onion soup, tripe, grilled pigs feet or snails at such bistrots as the Pied de Cochon, Au Chien Qui Fume, and Le Père Tranquille.

Gone since the war are the days when men and women in evening dress picked their way among the fragrant crates of watercress, the baskets of

mushrooms, the structures of fruit, the carpets of leeks, the barrows called diables, but tourists and other night owls still rub elbows in the cafés with butchers in bloody white smocks, porters and women vendors in aprons, truckers, and farmers. The "name" bistrots will stay on, hopefully. The little bars are staying, hopelessly. Few owners could afford the rent at the Howard Johnson-style cafés implanted in the new market at Rungis.

The exodus also brings to an end a centuries-old guild called the Corporation des Forts des Halles, a body of strong men—they competed for membership by carrying 220-pound weights through a pavilion—who served the dual function of porters and checkweighmen, policing the delivery of merchandise. Stevedoring companies will move goods at Rungis. The women of Les Halles had the privilege of haranguing the king once a year; the tradition is perpetuated by a delegation of porters and shopwomen to the Elysées Palace on May 1, bringing a posy of lilies of the valley. Who will carry on the tradition nobody knows.

The end of Les Halles is also the end for thousands of casual laborers and other "little people," and for many of the 1200 regular merchants and brokers. Nearly one-third have chosen to take government indemnities and retire or join other firms. Among the rest, there has been a wave of mergers, aimed at meeting the higher costs of large-scale modern operation at Rungis, complete with computer billing and closed-circuit television.

Nearly everybody agreed that Les Halles had to go. It was, said Gaston Benoit, an oldtime importer, a "daily miracle" to move the food for the metropolis in and out of Les Halles, which choked some 70 acres in the center of Paris. Rungis covers 1400 acres. Everybody agreed, but many are now having second thoughts. It is widely feared that the Orly-to-Paris traffic problem, already critical, will become impossible.

4

The small grocers and chefs of Paris, who used to find all they needed within 200 yards at Les Halles, may now find Rungis too vast and too distant. Thus Mr. Benoit feared that Rungis, which was to concentrate and so reduce the number of intermediaries between farmer and consumer, would actually create new intermediaries—agents and demiwholesalers—to serve this market, at a higher price and probably a loss in quality.

Mr. Benoit feared that the "great gamble of Rungis," a government investment of upwards of $100 million based on American marketing experience, might have come too late. The big chain stores, buying directly from the farmers, and the sale of produce by sample and description rather than direct handling, may be making the market obsolete. A casualty in the process, he added, may be all the individuality of the old system. "The consumer is being conditioned," Mr. Benoit said. "He will lose all freedom of choice."

What will happen to Les Halles nobody knows. Last year, the city presented six architects' plans for rebuilding the quarter on grandiose modern lines, with offices, hotels, garages, theaters, and stadium. They caused an uproar of protests, and were dropped. Pending a new one, the city is limiting itself to a drive to poison the rats of Les Halles, before famine drives them into the surrounding quarter.

"I'm glad it's going," said Gérard Jarry, a young barman in the Latin Quarter. "The traffic jams, the dirt. When I drive home in the afternoon, when the flower market is on, I've got to take a wide detour." Like many other Parisians, Mr. Jarry likes to drive out to Orly airport on weekends, to dine and watch the planes take off. He said he might try the new cafés at Rungis, too.

Mrs. Doy, the librarian who walks to work through Les Halles, shook her head sadly. "These young people," she concluded, "don't know how to live."

THE NEW HALLES

The struggle for Les Halles, "the belly of Paris," was lost over the issue of traffic. When I was there recently, the traffic was indeed gone from Les Halles, and most of its unforgettable life as well. The site was a wasteland of rubble and excavation for buildings whose nature has not yet been clearly defined.

At dawn that day, André Allard, the bistrot-keeper, drove to Rungis to do his biweekly shopping. He used to shop Les Halles every day, but hardly any restaurateur or retailer does that any more; most, in fact, shop by telephone, and a whole network of commission buyers and semiwholesalers has sprung up to serve them. Further, Mr. Allard no longer shops for produce at Rungis, because the fruit and vegetable handlers there decided to open their market in the afternoons. That way, they get to sleep nights, like everybody else. But the produce arrives in the city stores and restaurants in the evening, putting a grave burden on the retailers' storage capacity, and adding another day to the age of berries, fruit, and vegetables consumed by Parisians.

En route, Mr. Allard commented on the ease with which his station wagon rolled on deserted roadways. (Coming back during the morning rush hour was something else again, despite a road especially built for Rungis.) Easily again, he passed through the toll gate with a commuting ticket—admission to the public costs roughly 70 cents—and parked in an ample lot beside the huge fish shed.

Any food market is an exciting place, and Rungis is no exception, with dealers haggling among the gorgeous piles of foodstuffs, while computer-directed scoreboards overhead record arrivals and prices. But the Formica-and-neon cafés were, as Mr. Allard observed, a sad replacement for the little bistrots of Les Halles, where truckers and dealers shouted happily over their morning rabbit stew or breaded pig's feet and Beaujolais. "The only advantage here," grumbled one middle-aged fish broker, "is that I find a parking place."

A husky young wholesaler retorted that "the battle has been won" at Rungis, because provincial buyers were coming into the market who had never made their way to Les Halles. When the question of the relative quality and cost of food was raised, however, the young dealer turned grave. He mentioned the recent introduction of salmon raised in shallow coastal pens in Denmark and in Brittany. "They have soft flesh," he said. "No good. But it's coming. It'll

be like chicken. Chicken got to the point where people wouldn't eat it, and the growers had to turn back, now this problem is passing over into beef and fish. They're talking of raising sea bass!"

This sentimental visitor recalled the unforgettable scene at Les Halles every morning at 9 o'clock, when the wholesale market ended and the buyers retreated to the bistrots. A gong would ring, the gates would open and the public would swarm in, sacks swinging, to buy what had been left unsold. Now, the leftovers go back into the ample refrigerators at Rungis. "I had a box of Danish sole not long ago that stood in the frigo for 15 days and was still fresh," the young wholesaler said darkly. He was asked what was wrong with that. "It's not natural," he said impatiently. "I suppose they're putting antibiotics in the ice."

To sum up, it may be that the battle for Rungis has been won, in the sense that it is a going concern and that, while many small dealers have retired or gone bankrupt as a result of the higher cost of operations there, the surviving firms seem to be thriving. But the answer to the question posed here is negative:

Paris eats less well and pays more for it, because it destroyed Les Halles.

7

ALL RIGHT, SO YOU HEARD A SEAL BARK

Paris—April, 1966

Three trained seals wearing napkins gulped raw fish before television cameras in the Rue Saint Benoit this morning to symbolize what is to come for Saint-Germain-des-Prés and its hungry visitors. The seals had been engaged to publicize the latest of a series of ultramodern, gimmicky establishments that are springing up in this old quarter of the Left Bank, once the haunt of monks and scholars, then of artists and writers, and now of tourists. The new place is called the Bistingo (pronounced *beestango*), a coinage from bistrot and distingué. Among its gimmicks will be broiled seafood and brass nozzles built into the walls, like the air-conditioning vents of airliners.

The promoters of the Bistingo plan to pipe in upon the clientele a perfumed atmosphere redolent of sea air, to promote the appetite for fish, and enriched with pure oxygen, to promote euphoria.

The new wave broke upon the Place Saint-Germain-des-Prés last summer with the opening of Le Drugstore, diagonally across from the famous Romanesque church tower. Le Drugstore is an emporium-diner-movie house in a brassy decor which caricatures the Belle Epoque or Gay Nineties, and which has been called the most hideous thing in Paris. It has been a smash hit.

A syndicate with even bigger ideas moved into the quarter. For a starter, it bought an old restaurant nearby and engaged the designer of Le Drugstore to tear out the genuine Belle Epoque fittings and install a neo-Belle Epoque decor. The place was dubbed Le Bistrot de Paris to indicate that it would be THE bistrot of Paris and to satisfy a penchant of the syndicate for names beginning with "B."

One of the partners was Roland Pozzo di Borgo, a leader in the advertising business, and the promotion was a triumph for the trade. Even before Le Bistrot opened last autumn, the gossip columns were studded with the names of celebrities who were determined to eat there. Since then it's been hard to buy a seat.

The guiding spirit of Le Bistrot was Michel Oliver, a tense, darkly handsome man of 34, who until then had managed his father's great restaurant, the Grand Véfour. "I quit the Véfour," Mr. Oliver told a visitor, "to prove I could do something different." The visitor commented that he had made his point, and asked why he didn't stop to catch his breath. "The Bistrot will always be what it is," Mr. Oliver replied. "If I stay here

I'll die like a fish with its mouth open. One must go on all the time, all the time, all the time."

He strode around the corner, stopped to embrace a lady acquaintance, and pushed through a crowd of photographers into the Bistingo. One of his partners, the nightclub operator Maurice Casanova, was broiling pink ocean crayfish over a gas flame and passing them around, demanding, "Isn't it delicious?" A bystander tasted one and commented, "Burning fish is not cuisine."

Oliver took his visitor out, past the Brocherie next door—a meat-broiling shop—and into the Bilboquet, a nightclub on the corner, where he signed a stack of checks. Then a few steps on to a printing plant on the corner, which workmen were already gutting for the syndicate's next project. This will be a plant with seats for 900 diners, a large food bar with vending machines on the ground floor, and a basement movie. The syndicate is thinking of calling it Le Bidule, a word in argot which may be translated as the thing, but is more precisely a euphemism for bordello. An associate said, "Do you realize how many people will be coming to Saint Germain in

the spring, with money in their pockets, not knowing what to do?"

"You understand, the problem of Saint Germain," Oliver said, "is that the mass of clientele always eat badly. They don't know how to eat. They just push any door. You can give them a steak. That's unthinkable to me, because it's been done. I must do something new."

Following Le Bidule will come three more establishments already located, and scores more in the planning. Mr. Oliver has also been approached by American syndicates, one of which, he says, wants him to build a chain in the United States.

"I'll go," he said, "when I'm big enough to be on an equal footing with them."

TWO BEEHIVES OF ART

Paris—November, 1965

Across half the width of Paris, two human beehives now stand, one a crumbling slum redolent with misery and faded glory, the other a gleaming antiseptic box. They present a vivid contrast between the lives of struggling artists before and after public philanthropy chose to lend a hand.

The older hive is a small round building, three stories high, with a roof like a coolie's hat coming to a point in a cupola. It began as the wine pavilion at the Paris Exposition of 1900. The sculptor Alfred Boucher, himself comfortably successful, dreamed a dream of housing other creative souls in a community. He bought the pavilion and moved it to a wasteland on the Passage de Dantzig, facing the Vaugirard slaughterhouse near the Porte de Versailles, on the southwestern edge of the city.

Remaining materials from the exposition went to form a surrounding cluster of studios and a theater, and the whole complex was christened

with pomp, Villa Médicis. But it soon received the name it still is known by, La Ruche—the Beehive —from the shape of the central building. The three floors around a central well were lined with tiny cells, which were assigned to artists at low rents, which they frequently neglected to pay. Plumbing was, and remains, almost nonexistent —a leaking faucet on each floor and two latrines which flank the sculptured entry and announce their presence through the house.

One of the "bees," the painter Jacques Chapiro, has written a moving memoir of life in La Ruche, with its rare ecstasies and ever-present agonies. In the summertime, the smells of the slaughterhouse invaded those of the vermin-infested hive. In the winter, the freezing drafts were feebly resisted by a few wood or alcohol stoves and candles, and even these were often beyond the means of the tenants. Yet the dubious shelter of La Ruche was gladly shared by hundreds of impoverished artists, most of them

10

now forgotten, but some bearing names such as Marc Chagall, Fernand Léger, Chaim Soutine, Archipenko, and Modigliani.

For a time, it is said, several of Chagall's paintings were used to cover a rabbit hutch, and some of Modigliani's to replace broken panes. One day, Chapiro recounts, the famished Soutine was

in his studio, studying a herring on a stool, unable to decide whether to eat it or to paint it, when a rat boldly made off with it.

The dirty, hungry artists were outcasts then, in a state of mutual hostility with prosperous society. Chapiro says that a dealer, tired of the pleas for help from a desperate painter, sent him a rope with a note, "You will have to find your own hook."

The founder, Boucher, died in 1934. Ugly apartment houses and garages rose around the colony, hiding it from sight. The theater had long before gone to feed the little stoves, and weeds grew around the statuary abandoned on every side. But La Ruche still stands or rather sags, all its cells occupied—some of them by a new generation of struggling artists. Uninvited visitors are not welcome, as a sign on one cell door emphatically declares. Until World War II, young artists from all over the world put up with conditions such as those in La Ruche because it seemed impossible to them to work anywhere but in Paris. This belief is no longer prevalent. Thus it was not only sympathy for the artist but a recognition that Paris was fading as a world art center that caused state, city, and private agencies to promote the Cité Internationale des Arts.

The building, just completed on the right bank of the Seine facing the Île St. Louis, is a great concrete and glass slab, with long straight corridors like those in a Surrealist movie, the whole looking as if it were designed by a computer and stamped out by a machine. Yet it comfortably houses 135 artists—five fewer than those in the tiny complex of La Ruche in its heyday. Tenants of the new hive, who come from more than 20 countries, live in neatly furnished living-bedroom-studios, the sculptors in high ceilinged ones on the lower levels, the painters in the middle and the musicians on the top floor, the fifth. Each studio has an easel or piano, a daybed, a modern bathroom, and a tiny kitchen with a single hotplate and no refrigerator. For here, as at La

Ruche, the assumption seems to be that the artist like the worker bee must be a celibate.

Different times, different surroundings produce different art. The dying La Ruche still suggests something of the gaiety of its origin as a wine pavilion at a fair, a far cry from the bleak new artists' Hilton by the Seine. Surely none of the old bees would have hesitated to move into the new hive. Whether the art created here will be as great or as human remains to be seen.

THE DEMISE OF THE REAR PLATFORM

Paris—February, 1971

The sprint for the rear platform has vanished from the Paris street scene after 90-odd more or less glorious years. When the first horsedrawn omnibus appeared on the boulevards in 1879, the platform was there to receive boarders, with its uniformed ticket puncher or half a dozen male travelers ready with a helping hand for a pretty girl. Athletic types, young and not so young, took nonchalant satisfaction in overtaking a rolling bus and swinging aboard, undoing the safety chain, and in hopping off in midstreet, facing forward and running.

More staid Parisians loved to ride the platform to admire the passing scene, breathe the fragrance of the season (in days when each season did have its fragrance), and perhaps smoke a reflective pipe, like Georges Simenon's detective, le Commissaire Maigret, whose pocket was picked one day by a murderer on a rear platform, en route to the Quai des Orfèvres.

Nevertheless, the last rear-platform bus rolled its last run on the 21 line. It is a good route for saying farewell to Paris: Gare St. Lazare, Opéra, Louvre, Pont Neuf (Notre Dame to the left), Boulevard St. Michel, Luxembourg, Rue de Gay Lussac (of the 1968 barricades) . . . and on to Gentilly. Gently. Gently, indeed. For buses can seldom roll fast in Paris these days; they do well to maintain the pace of the old horse carts. That, is one reason why the platform had to go. "It was very pleasant, I admit it," said Henri Clausse, a spokesman for the transit system. "It was also convenient to be able to step down anywhere. But it is no longer possible."

The city began gradually replacing its 1936 rear-platform Renaults with closed buses in 1950, on safety grounds, it was said. However, it is also steadily replacing the *receveur*, or ticket collector, in favor of the one-man bus with a single entry up front and slot machines for tickets. The platform bus requires the second man. Economy is necessary because buses, as anyone can see, roll nearly empty most of the time (when they are not stuck in traffic). "It is a vicious circle," said Jean

13

Robert, founder of the Musée des Transports Urbains. "People don't ride the buses because the service is bad. The service is bad because people don't ride the buses."

They ride their own cars, instead, and they often take over the lanes newly reserved to public transport. Mr. Robert said it was a matter of inadequate enforcement. In any case, the platform has quit Paris, and is not likely to return. To a sentimentalist who suggested that perhaps one day the city would be inspired to bring it back, as when it recently bought a fleet of new doubledecker buses, Mr. Clausse replied sadly that there was little chance it would repeat that venture. The novelty of riding the doubledecker has worn off, he reported, and the new Imperiales are rolling with no better occupancy than the others. And they take a two-man crew.

"We are losing several million travelers a year," Mr. Clausse said. "Finally, we will have to do as you do in New York, making motoring so burdensome that people will take buses."

WHAT ESCAPED THE WAR
DID NOT ALWAYS SURVIVE

Paris—July, 1967

Tourists visiting Cognac used to detour through the village of Baignes to admire its medieval covered markets. To provide them with parking space, the village fathers tore down the markets. Now there is plenty of space, but no tourists. . . .

A little Gothic chapel at St. Riquier, in Picardy, in which Joan of Arc was held prisoner, is now used to store potatoes. . . . A highway engineer in southern France came across a group of Gallo-Roman tombs; fearing a delay to his project if he told the authorities, he had the tombs jack-hammered into crushed stone for his roadbed. . . .

In Brittany, a subprefect decided that a menhir, one of those great stones erected in rows by the ancient Druids, would be just the thing for his Japanese garden. His contractor uprooted half a dozen to choose one of them and crushed the rest.

In Senlis, a handsome but neglected walled town near Paris, five abandoned Gothic churches are used, respectively, as a garage, a market, a dancehall, a movie house, and a school. . . . In Paris, the last vestige of a twelfth-century convent, the refectory, is used as a firehouse. . . .

Man's destruction of his heritage is not new. What is new, in France, is a truly popular movement to defend it—a movement founded almost accidentally by Pierre de Lagarde, a young reporter for the government broadcast network.

It began with a two-minute radio spot five years ago, in which Mr. de Lagarde recounted the illegal sale of valuable relics by the village of Allouville-Bellefosse in Normandy. Statues were later recovered, but an entire church was lost forever;

it had been demolished for building materials. "Forty listeners wrote in," Mr. de Lagarde recalled in an interview. "They said, 'Come on out our way —the same thing is happening.'" A new career was born. But it was no bed of roses.

"I decided it was not enough to talk about esthetic values," Mr. de Lagarde said. "I set out to sensitize public opinion by creating a scandal. I started out with the mayor of ———. He called up and said he'd have my hide. Then I attacked the subprefect who dug up those menhirs. Prefects called Paris. I was off the air for two months. I have to spend a lot of my time pulling strings. I've had my program suppressed six times, been sued for slander five times. It never came to trial." The program, called "Masterpieces in Danger," became a popular television feature. A handsome illustrated "Guide to Masterpieces in Danger," just published, lists 2000 case studies and incidentally offers a tourist's handbook to neglected beauty.

World War II was, of course, a major destroyer of archaeological treasures—not always unavoidably. During the Normandy fighting, Mr. de Lagarde said, the Germans carefully destroyed the Abbaye de Lessay (since rebuilt); while at Valognes, the United States Army engineers bulldozed an early Gothic church to straighten a road. What escaped the war did not always survive the reconstruction. Bombs flattened Lisieux, leaving its flamboyant Gothic cathedral rising above the ruins. The carved woodwork of half a hundred old houses around it, which might have been salvaged, went to heat the town hall.

"People often favor destroying their old quarters because they associate them with slums and prostitution," Mr. de Lagarde said. "As if it were the fault of the architecture!"

He pins his hopes on an aroused public opinion. More and more these days, he is able to report victories as well as defeats. In Picardy, Maurice Duton left his craft, enamelwork, to stop the demolition of the Château de Guise. Gradually, he built up a team of young volunteers who are doing restoration work. Another group arose similarly near Château Thierry, led by Pierre Pottier. A devoted band of amateurs, including Americans, mapped the hidden treasures of the old Marais quarter of Paris, and put an ordinance through protecting it from further ravages.

The wrecker's ball, the bulldozer, and the concrete mixer are still making their inroads on the French scene. But their blitz is meeting resistance now.

THE FALLEN POPLARS

The tree-lined roads, the shady squares that long have symbolized France have been succumbing steadily to the demands of the automobile. The government decided to speed the process in the name of highway safety and has ordered the removal of trees from hundreds of miles of national routes. The results are already apparent. Travelers in search of the scenes painted by Corot have remarked many a stump along the way and many a village square razed for parking. In Paris itself, hundreds of great chestnuts have vanished from along the Seine, where an auto expressway was built, and squares excavated for underground garages. The new concrete surfaces, broken by ventilators, are too shallow for big trees to grow again.

The new measure is the most ambitious attack on the tree in recent French memory. Ironically, it transpires at the same time as the announcement by President Georges Pompidou of a 100-point program for the defense of nature, involving five ministries and all the departments of France.

The decision on the trees actually was taken months ago. The government was deeply concerned about the growing highway accident rate, and with reason. Deaths in 1970 approached 15,000, and with relation to population this was estimated to be by far the worst in Europe. The most notable results of a winter of safety discussions were the imposition of a national speed limit and the adoption of a blood test for alcoholism. The speed limit was put at 69 miles an hour with a tolerance of 82 miles for passing. And the alcohol test was watered down by the wine lobby; it may be administered only after a serious accident, and the penalty for a first offense or a modest degree of drunkenness is only a fine.

Unnoticed in the safety program was a decision "to suppress lateral obstacles." This meant anything within five feet of the roadway—ditches, walls and, above all, trees. The chore was assigned to the Ministry of Equipment and Transportation, whose chief, Albin Chalandon, has been quoted as saying, "I am not a fanatic about green spaces." He is now embroiled with conservationists over his effort to cut an autoroute through the Parc de St. Cloud and open the green belt beyond it to housing developments.

The assumption that when an automobile hits a tree it's the tree's fault is quintessentially French. Efforts to control speed and drinking under the same safety program met strong opposition, and the program itself showed a certain ambivalence: its stated goal was to promote not only traffic safety but also fluidity— that is, speed. A leading conservationist here expressed surprise when advised of the decision.

He predicted there would be serious opposition when the news got around. But against the nature lovers will be the defenders of the right to drive 69 miles an hour down a country road—or 82, when passing.

21

THE PASSING OF A WAY OF LIFE

Marseille-les-Aubigny—May, 1971

In the dawning age of the supersonic boom, the muffled clip-clop of hooves on the towpath has vanished into memory. A traveler in the Loire Valley who paused here the other day, hoping to photograph the last horse-drawn barge in France, was told by a sympathetic lock-tender, "Ah, it was laid up last fall." Centuries of a certain way of life thus came to an end almost unnoticed, one day in September, when the *Atlas*, pulled by two mules, arrived from Monceau-les-Mines, some 48 miles away, with 150 tons of coal. After that, all cargo on French waterways would be pushed or pulled by engines.

The traveler slipped away without trying to renew an acquaintance with René Besle, the last independent towbargeman on the Berry Canal. Some months earlier, he had had a painful talk with Mr. Besle and his wife on their boat, the *Sirius*. The black barge, with a team of horses on

deck and spotless living quarters aft, had been tied up waiting for a cargo for two months, and the Besles sensed already that it would never come. The *Atlas*, a company boat, was still working. The soft sunlight of the Loire bathed the poplars and the silent hamlet beside the canal. But the middle-aged couple, stocky and brown from the sun, in blue denims and wooden sabots, were bitter.

"There is work for the big boats, yes, but not for us," Mr. Besle said. "It's the trucks that are changing everything. The small canals are all closed. It's all roads. It's nothing."

Actually, a canal supervisor observed later, the big waterways, capable of handling 700-ton motor barges to 3000-ton strings of barges, are thriving. He acknowledged that small feeder canals, like railroad spur lines, had been often falling into disuse, and that local promoters were eager to turn canal beds into expressways in Paris, Toulouse, and Dijon. Beauty lovers have so far held them off; in fact, the canal at Toulouse is being improved. "The canal is economic without a doubt," the supervisor said. "It's far cheaper to maintain than the railroad. The canals of the Midi, built by Louis XIV and never changed, are still rendering enormous service. There are not enough boats to meet the demand."

But they are big boats, to be sure. For the Besles, both of whom were born on barges, both of whom remember when there were 400 of their clan on the Berry Canal alone, it was the end. They recalled with bitter pride how hard a life it really was. Except for the five holidays a year on which canal traffic stops, every day was the same. They would rise an hour before dawn to tend the horses. At daylight, Mr. Besle would lead them down a gangplank sometimes slippery with rain or frost. Then until nightfall, he would drive them along the path, his wife holding the huge rudder or occasionally making it fast while she cooked or did chores. "Our parents sent us ashore to kinfolk when we were little," she said, "but we sent our children to boarding school. Ah, it was tough indeed, yes."

"In the fog and rain, we don't stop," Mr. Besle said. "When we're sick, we dose ourselves and

walk just the same—not like factory people, who get a little cold and stop working for five days. We made a living—not much, but we lived happy, anyhow." Mr. Besle said he had never thought of buying a motor barge—a new one would cost $55,000, he explained—and anyhow, "We're too old now." His wife agreed, "It's finished for us."

The canal supervisor said all the former bargemen were as bitter and nostalgic as the Besles. "In a factory," he explained, "they do whatever the foreman tells them to do. On the canal, they were their own bosses." He paused and added thoughtfully, "It was an illusion, to be sure."

24

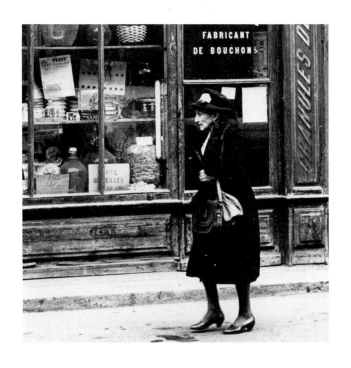

Part Two   **EN PROVINCE**

THE YEAR OF THE MILLENNIUM

Mont-St.-Michel—December, 1966

This was the year of the millennium, the year the monks returned, the year of brilliant processions, the year when a record stream of pilgrims crossed the sands to the Gothic spires of Mont-St.-Michel. But here it will long be recalled as the year the Mayor put the itching powder in Miss Joliet's desk. He also scrambled her papers, cut her telephone line, threw stench bombs into her office, soaked her chair with icewater, and finally mailed her a tiny coffin. For all this Mayor Alain Auvray, a souvenir merchant, received a three months' suspended sentence and a $300 fine.

These unusual events had a common origin: the decision of the Government to celebrate the thousandth anniversary of the mount, to reinstall a dozen monks in the abbey for the season, and to appoint Antoinette Joliet of Paris, a Catholic lay leader, to organize the celebration.

Actually, the mount became a shrine early in the eighth century, following an apparition of St. Michael. But the sponsors counted back 1,000 years to the arrival of Benedictines, replacing an earlier order of monks who had fallen into disrepute. After a great era of pilgrimage and construction, the Benedictines themselves fell into disrepute and in the eighteenth century the abbey was turned into a royal prison.

In 1874 the Government began reconstructing it, and the towers rising dramatically out of the bay have been a magnet for travelers ever since.

The millennium festivities swelled the total for the season to 600,000. On a typical Sunday last August, 11,000 came. In a hot, sticky mass they jammed the single narrow Grande Rue along the cliff, those descending struggling to pass those going up, and all of them being cajoled by souvenir merchants, restaurant pullers-in, and barkers for the three so-called "museums" crying "The visit to Mont-St.-Michel begins here." Three times that day, scuffles broke out and gendarmes had to intervene.

One might have expected the merchants to be pleased at the festival plan. Their reaction was quite different.

"I can understand them a little," said Brother Joseph, one of the monks. "They must earn their living between June 1 and Sept. 1. They had only one fear, that the monks would engage in business. Actually, we were very well received by the inhabitants. The only difficulty was with the Village Hall. When the millennium committee moved in, friction was inevitable. The Mayor took a 'grippe' against Miss Joliet. You know, Auvray is a socialist and a bit of what we call a priest-eater, but he is a *brave homme*."

The words *brave homme*—fine chap—were applied to Auvray also by two men who appeared to be the only residents of the mount not associated with the tourist business. One was the slender, white-haired village priest, who, asked for his name, replied smilingly, "I just call myself the curé of Mont-St.-Michel."

"Auvray," the priest said, "is a brave homme, very devoted but a little impulsive. He worked hard to renovate the town hall. It was for him, how shall I say, vexing to see it taken over by the

secretary of the millennium committee. Miss Joliet was . . ." he laughed "a force." Adding to the trouble, he said, was a rumor that the Government was going to install a snack bar in the abbey.

The priest agreed that there were abuses in commercialism that should be cleaned up, especially the "museums," but he added that not all visitors were interested in the abbey, and for these the souvenir shops and restaurants served a function. "At least they see the mount," he said. "Even in the Middle Ages they sold to pilgrims here."

Constant Beaufils, the local lifeboat captain and the last active fisherman still living on the mount, is another friend of the Mayor. He commented, "If there was an election, Auvray would win by a big majority." (There are only about 80 voters in the community, among the 50 families, most of whom leave the mount during the winter.) "The monks," Beaufils insisted, "wanted to open a souvenir shop here. And the Government wants to cut off the dike and the footwalk. That would force tourists to wait two hours for a ferry. They would take snapshots and depart."

Auvray himself, a tall, gray-haired man in a fisherman's cap, willingly talked about the affair in his souvenir shop on the rampart. Chain smoking hand-rolled cigarettes, he spoke bitterly about Miss Joliet ("she came in like a meteor and took over the Mairie, and we were nobody"), but saw his conviction as part of his long struggle with the authorities over the dike. In scholarly pamphlets, Auvray had agreed that the encroachment of sand upon the mount was an esthetic tragedy, but argued that the cause was not the dike but the withdrawal of water for mainland use from a stream that used to wash around it. He wants the Government to turn back the water, make a broad moat around the mount and build a foot tunnel under it for tourists. As for the monks, he declared: "The taxpayers have spent fabulous sums to restore the abbey. Now it's finished and they come and say 'It's ours.' I am for separation of church and state."

Now the monks have ended their visit. Whether they will return, Brother Joseph said, depends on the Government, on the diocese, and on whether the religious orders can find monks to live here. Meanwhile, the wind whips down the empty Grande Rue, the sand drifts higher in the bay, and the green meadows along the mainland gradually spread toward this sometime island, now becoming a peninsula.

THE WAR OF THE BODY SNATCHERS

Freyming-Merlebach–December, 1971

It has been three months since the last unseemly row over a coffin in Freyming-Merlebach. A truce appears to have been imposed in La Guerre des Croque-Morts. The terms of the armistice between two rival undertakers are a mystery. People of this border town do not like to talk about it. They feel they are being made fun of by "the interior," as the people of Alsace and Lorraine call the rest of France.

In similar circumstances elsewhere undertakers have been just as underhanded. In Perpignan, at the opposite end of France, a funeral director was

arrested last month for putting hidden microphones in a rival establishment so as to get to a death scene first.

A trade war in the funeral business is a rare and new development in France, nonetheless, for traditionally death has been a quiet community affair. French law made undertaking a public utility, assigned first to the parish church and now to the town, but most communities prefer to hand the chore to a concessionnaire, who pays a small tax for the monopoly and agrees to abide by a moderate price scale and to bury paupers free. He is colloquially known as a croque-mort, from an ancient term meaning to cause the dead to disappear.

Freyming-Merlebach is a special case. In fact, it was two towns, each with about 9000 souls, until last February, when they merged—not from any sense of identity, but because they felt that together they could swing more weight with Paris in getting much-needed economic help. Although to the stranger it seems to be one bleak, sprawling mining town, the residents have never seen it that way.

The Freyming Merchants Association declined to promote a parade that would lead its customers toward the Merlebach shopping center—and vice versa. Each half of Freyming-Merlebach still has its own fire company, its own Chamber of Commerce, and its own undertaker. This should never have posed any problem but for one thing: The social administration of the Lorraine coal basin built its hospital in Freyming, just over the line from Merlebach.

All the witnesses to what followed are anonymous, at their request, though the facts are not disputed. First, people for 30 miles around stopped dying at home. Of the 600 deaths reported each year in Freyming-Merlebach, about 400 are recorded in the hospital. At an average of $400 or so for a funeral, "it's a substantial market," a town authority observed ruefully. Since

anyone who died in Freyming was assigned by law to the funeral monopoly there, the local firm, Pompes Funèbres Sogne-Dôme, grew mightily. By the same token, Merlebach's concern, a branch of the nationwide Pompes Funèbres Générales, saw its business dwindle to 60 burials a year.

Seven years ago the hospital built a cardiac wing—in Merlebach. The Merlebach concern claimed all the dead, but Sogne-Dôme retorted that the patients were admitted in Freyming and left that way. The war was on. A death would start a race for the body and the first team on hand would usually get it. But the owner of Sogne-Dôme, Mrs.

31

Marie Madeleine Sogne-Dôme, would not permit what she regarded as her property to be stolen. In one celebrated scene last summer, she sat determinedly on an occupied coffin in the courtyard and refused to leave. On another memorable occasion, Mrs. Sogne-Dôme called outside gendarmes, unfamiliar with the situation, to report the theft of a corpse. She led them in a raid on a wake in Freyming, which ended in some confusion.

Recently the story reached the press and the town fathers decided that it was the last straw.

They voted to cancel both concessions when they expire next spring. The Mayor, Charles Metzinger, had a talk with the rival undertakers: what he told them is not known, but there have been no scandals since.

A merger is in the logic of things, but people here doubt that Mrs. Sogne-Dôme would agree. Nor do they think that she should be squeezed out in favor of a big corporation. "Sogne-Dôme is, after all, a representative of independent handicraft, which is dying," a town official remarked in all seriousness.

A GIRL WITHOUT A NAME

Plessis-Grimault—November, 1966

Yannick and Charlotte Duclos called their first baby Yvon and their second Soazic, both good Breton names. The third child they did not name —a Norman court did. It ordered that the daughter born to the Duclos on August 21, 1965, be named Mikelaig. The order has just been upheld by an appeals court in nearby Caen and Yannick Duclos, a slight, bearded young technician at a French television transmitter on a lonely hilltop here, said afterwards he could not afford to carry the fight further. So as soon as the decree is properly stamped and registered, the 15-month-old girl will come into legal existence and receive the birth certificate that must serve her for life, as Mikelaig Patricia Duclos.

But at home, Duclos declared, he could continue to call the little girl Kelig. This is a fond diminutive for Kel, which in turn is a diminutive for Mikel. Irish equivalents are Mickey, Mike, and Michael. The similarity is not coincidental, since the Bretons are Celts and speak a language closely related to the Gaelic and Celtic still surviving in Ireland and parts of Great Britain. Thus Patricia is a common Breton name, and so is Patrik, without the "c." A recommended list of Breton given names published in Rennes includes, for boys, Arthur, Conan, Fagan, Magloire (pronounced Maguire, almost), Morgan, and Tristan, and for girls, Yseult, Tristane, Guinievre, Mai and Marig (equivalents of Mary), Yvonne (the name of Madame de Gaulle), and Kelig.

Yvon, the name of the first Duclos child, is Breton for John, and Soazic means Françoise. When the third came along, the Duclos read the list again, and Kelig took their fancy. The district registration officer, however, was not at all pleased. Historically, as Mr. Duclos explained, with weary good humor, children could be christened only with saints' names until the French Revolution. Then all limitations were lifted, but when patriots began giving their babies such names as "Mort aux Bourbons," the curbs were reimposed. Since then, names have generally been picked from calendars of saints' days, the Breton calendar included.

A decree by the Ministry of Justice last May gave registry offices permission also to accept names current in the Basque, Breton, and Provençal tongues and in foreign countries. But this came after Yannick Duclos' encounter with the registrar. Anyhow, the official said, Kelig was

not a proper name but a nickname at that. The registrar refused to write down Kelig and Duclos refused to propose another name, even when gendarmes came to his home to persuade him.

One handicap Duclos faced was that like many other young Bretons, he had emigrated to find a job, and so he had to put his case before Normans.

Another was that the Breton language appears to be rather ambiguous about feminine endings. A name may be both masculine and feminine or may become feminine by addition of "e," "a," or "ig." To some purists, the feminine ending "a" is not Breton but a snobbish importation from the French.

The court decided to take the Duclos option, Kelig, and build it into a proper name, such as Mikelig, and then insert an "a" just to make clear that the Duclos baby was a girl. Hence, Mikelaig (pronounced mee-kel-eyeg). The form has raised eyebrows of Breton scholars, who consider it a French legal fiction. But under that name Mikelaig Patricia (Kelig) Duclos will henceforth live.

And one day soon, a man with a leather pouch will bicycle up to the door and count out to Mrs. Duclos some $300 in retroactive family allowance for a third child who was born 15 months ago but has just become a citizen.

PATRONYMICALLY HANDICAPPED

Paris—November, 1968

The Association of the Patronymically Handicapped held its annual meeting at Lens in northern France this month. Only two persons attended: the founder, Jean Meurdesoif, whose patronym means "I'm dying of thirst," and a man named Cocu.

Meurdesoif said fear of ridicule had kept away sundry Messrs. Salope (slob), Pourceau (swine), Grossetête (fathead), and others whose names do not often appear in newspapers of general circulation.

The association wants the procedure for changing names to be eased, and not only for people whose names are absurd at first glance. It cites a café keeper named Victor Hugo, who recalls school as one long ordeal and still complains that when other boys were getting bicycles, he was getting the works of Hugo as gifts—which he still has not read.

Meurdesoif recalled a woman whose grief was that she was not Madame Cochon. She broke off her engagement to a man of that name when her girlfriends congratulated her on all the piglets she would bring into the world. Now, she mourned, she was an old maid.

THE BACHELORS' FAIR

Esparros — May, 1966

The sightseers came by the thousands to the Bachelors' Fair of Esparros, in cars and buses, clogging the narrow mountain roads. Cupid never had a chance. Esparros is a hamlet lost in an idyllic valley under the shoulder of the Pyrenees in a land called Bigorre, where the men wear floppy berets and the women and cows work in the fields.

A hundred years ago, Esparros counted 800 people. Now there are 244. Most of them are named Duthu, and 27 are bachelors. The situation is no mystery nor even unusual in the Pyrenees. The girls go off to the lowlands, as they say here, to work in hotels or factories, and they never return. Some of the boys leave, too, but pride keeps many clinging to the family acres. Some of the acres are so steep that the men and women roll the hay down and then carry it on shoulder ricks to the barn.

Three months ago, Philippe Balagna, a dapper 69-year-old bachelor who had retired from banking to settle in Esparros, proposed a village

fair for the Pentecost weekend. It was to be a regional fête to introduce unmarried men and girls of the Bigorre in the hope that romance would flourish. What did flourish was publicity. The story flashed around the world. The regional chambers of commerce moved in and the villagers suddenly found themselves blinking in the glare of a vast, modern promotion. The mailman, Emile Duthu, putted in on his motorbike each day with a pouch of letters from lonely men and women of all ages as far off as New Zealand:

"I am very happy at the news. I am 58 and in excellent health." "I am rich, I earn 350 francs ($70) a month." "I am 52, I want somebody gay. I would like a sentimental man, above all not bald." A young man in Fontainebleau sent a heroic autobiography and said, "I will trade my liberty for a very large fortune." A young woman in Arlington, Virginia, said she would sell her 500 cows to marry the right man. Her letter was turned over to the bachelor mayor of an adjoining village.

In the village, carnival workers were setting up their tents and newsmen crowded the tiny square. Most of the villagers were in the fields cutting hay or plowing with teams of cows and oxen whose heads were covered with sheepskin. Outside their stone houses, worn women in black watched the scene in silence. A white-haired young woman, the mother of seven Duthus, with an eighth on the way, said she did not know why the fête was being held. She paused, her lip trembling, then said: "My faith, you know this life is hard. It must be better elsewhere."

A very old Madame Duthu said, "The young men should marry because the houses are falling. But I don't think much will come of it. Those women from Bordeaux and Toulouse, they won't take this painful life." A 20-year-old waitress in a nearby inn looking out on a hillside where three women were turning hay said, "Yes, I'd like to get married but not to a farmer." A bachelor of 65

hitched a 20-mile ride to the fair, cheerfully confident that he would find a wife much as he would find a cow at a cattle fair. Asked what kind he wanted, he replied, "Well, two women of 30 are better than one of 60."

Cars filled the meadows and backed up for many miles. Peasant families, townfolk, and a sportscar set wearing smoked glasses poured through the fields to see the fun. Barkers shouted,

loudspeakers blared, three orchestras played, and in the church tower small boys tirelessly rang bells that had seldom pealed for weddings. At one of the carnival sheds a packed crowd watched grinning jokers and grim-faced bachelors and spinsters register their availability. Each was given a red ribbon to wear and a private number that they were to use to identify one another. Many demanded to see their opposite numbers immediately and were disappointed to learn that they were on their own.

About 300 men, nearly all bronzed men of the Bigorre, had signed up by late afternoon and stepped back into the crowd. About 75 women had also braved or welcomed the cameras and stares. All were apparently city women, nearly all of them middle-aged.

The red-ribboned townswomen strolled around in pairs, and some found townsmen to talk to.

"It's pretty here now," one woman said, "but what's it like in the winter?"

Lost in the fringes of the crowd watching the dancers and bright noisy city people were little groups of silent, dark men in floppy berets, some of them wearing red ribbons. Nobody seemed to pay any attention to them.

BLOOD IN THE COCKPIT

Lille—March, 1969

The two miners met in the middle of the ring and cautiously held their birds beak to beak. The gray-gold cock pecked viciously, and the red pulled away. A dozen voices cried, "Mille francs le gris." —Two dollars on the gray. There were few takers, and they demanded odds. The owners placed their birds in opposite corners and left the ring.

The roosters, collars flaring, wings out, met above the center and came down—the red on top, with a two-inch steel spur in a wing of the gray. A pause, both birds breathing heavily. They parted, clashed again with a whoosh of feathers, came down, parted, and clashed again. Finally, they fell in a corner, the red still on top, gasping, unable to rise because a spur was caught in the breast of the gray. Three long minutes passed. A buzzer sounded and a light flashed on the rim of the wire fence around the ring. Match null. The owners glumly returned to the ring to remove their birds, both of them dying.

At the edge of the crowd, a husky redhead in a leather jacket earnestly demanded of a visiting reporter: "Do you think it's barbaric?"

The reporter, squinting at the feather-and-blood-specked ring, replied with an equivocal grimace.

In the bleak, gray mining country along the Belgian border, diversions are few: soccer, bicycle racing, and pigeon racing—often in the rain— and, indoors, boxing and cockfighting. The cockfighters are sensitive about outside opinion because their sport was outlawed in 1963, after bands of animal-lovers raided cockpits and smashed the rings. "They didn't even pay admission," an oldtimer said indignantly. The ban was informally lifted the following year, when councilmen of the two northern departments unanimously petitioned Paris for relief. Last fall, a Government decree made cockfighting legal in those areas where it was traditional—that is, the Flemish border country from Dunkirk to Valenciennes—as bullfighting is legal in the south of France. But no new "gallodromes" may be added.

Fear of the humane societies preserves an air of clandestinity about the fights, which are staged in backrooms of small-town cafés, with no publicity. The visit of a reporter and photographer was arranged on a pledge not to identify the site. Even so, their arrival stirred an angry dispute among the fans—a dispute which did not subside until the photographer left. Friendlier fans sought to persuade the visitors of the merits of their sport. They introduced a teacher in track togs, who affirmed that benefit cockfights helped pay for school equipment. René Turpin, a businessman who raises birds and judges combats, said there was no money to be gained in the sport except for the café keepers.

"If you break even at the end of the year," he asserted with feeling, "You're ahead."

Like cock breeders the world over, the locals insisted that their birds would rather fight than eat or make love. Gustav Dambach, a groundkeeper who with his brother Désiré keeps 40 cocks, said that in idleness a bird would suffer a bloodstroke—also known as false fire or the rage—from pure frustration. "I lost ten birds the year of the ban," he said.

The birds that fight in Flanders—clandestinely on the Belgian side, legally here—weigh 10 to 15 pounds, which is twice the size of those raised for combat in Britain, the United States, and Latin America. The three-inch curved blades worn

elsewhere are banned here in favor of the two-inch straight pin which, Désiré Dambach said, "kills quicker and with less pain." At the age of six months, a cockerel must be separated from his brothers because they would fight to the death. Their combs are trimmed off and they are penned up, with little exercise, until they are put into the ring at ten or eleven months, and at intervals thereafter if they survive.

Jules Desprez, a retired miner who was putting spurs on a red rooster named Zozo, looked shocked when asked if, like American cockfighters, he gave his birds a little whiskey before a fight. "Oh no!" he said, "we don't dope. If we did, the bird would die next day." Other breeders said sugar lumps soaked in gin or rum, and toasted croutons soaked in beer, were often beneficial.

A variety of medicaments is used to restore birds so they may fight again. The redheaded miner drew from a pocket a bottle labeled Le Contre-Coups de L'Abbé Pergrigeon, or Father Pergrigeon's Remedy Against Blows—a family medicine prescribed for both internal and external human use against "serious falls, violent blows, cerebral congestions, apoplexy, arthritis, gout, rheumatism, middle-age maladies, high blood pressure, liver trouble." The Dambach brothers, on the other hand, swear by a panacea called Avion marketed specifically for birds. They said they also used it on themselves, for cuts and bruises. If all treatment fails, the bird is eaten. Mr. Desprez said: "You use a little butter, onions, red wine, and cook gently for two hours—a coq au vin, quoi!"

During an intermission, as two small groups huddled around tables for a dice lottery game locally known as pat-a-trac, the redhead sought out the visitors again.

"I work on the coal face," he said. "It's the hardest job in the mine. I get to bed about 3 in the morning, damn tired. The birds wake me up at 6.

If it was a dog, I'd kill it. Instead, I get up and take care of my birds. Because I love it."

Parting, the redhead said his bird had lost and was dead.

"He was two years old," the miner said. "I raised him like a kid."

After a pause, the visitor asked whether the bird would appear on the miner's table next day.

"Yes," he replied, with a quizzical shrug, "It's a compensation."

THE NOTAIRE

The *notaire* is hardly a sympathetic figure in literature. Balzac, who had been a *clerc de notaire* (as were Voltaire and Alexandre Dumas père), left a grim and lasting portrait, reflected in a recent cabaret song about the notary, "With his cold eye, his li'l briefcase, his overcoat and his calculating air . . . Ah! how sad, sad, sad!"

A living contradiction to this picture is "the Lion of Gardanne" Maître Charles Favier, celebrated *raconteur et baroudeur*, a yarn spinner and scrapper. True, he is a Southerner and he is exceptional even in the Midi where he has occasionally been accused of conduct unbecoming the dignity of a notaire. It is a charge to which he enthusiastically subscribes.

A stocky, crewcut, youthful man of 69, Maître Favier works in a paneled study decorated with a score of lion statuettes, gifts from admirers in tribute to one of his exploits. A touring circus developed the unfortunate habit of slapping its posters over those of Maître Favier, announcing the auction of some estate. The notaire slapped a lien on the caravan, and collected damages. Legend, as it will, touched up the incident, which became a lien on a lion.

A greater exploit of this type occurred during Maître Favier's long feud with the French railway system. It seems to have begun during the Occupation, when food packages sent to the Faviers from the family farm were subject to pilfering at the depot; once, he says, truffles were replaced by stones, to make up the declared weight. The notaire gathered evidence, got a court judgment for damages, summoned a *huissier*, or bailiff—and *seized* the depot. The seizure was of course nominal, pending payment of the judgment, but the huissier gravely itemized everything down to the pen wipers, and warned the stationmaster that nothing could be moved. "Every day for four days," Maître Favier recalls nostalgically, "I went down to inspect my station. Finally, the man paid."

The feud did not stop there. The notaire admits to having taken a "wicked pleasure" in bugging the railroad, tangling it in its own red tape. He relates, for example, how he exhumed old regulations to demand that conductors provide spittoons and reserve a special compartment for persons carrying loaded firearms. In his case, it was an ancient musket, which he bore in his capacity as a voluntary gamewarden. The title draws a laugh because Maître Favier proudly claims descent from a long line of poachers. ("What is forbidden is what tastes best," he said dreamily.)

Maître Favier delights in taking the stuffing out of the shirts of his fellow notaires, especially city ones. In Marseilles one day after the war, the brethren were putting away a splendid black-market lunch in a private salon when he telephoned to announce that he was a Communist reporter and was coming in with a photographer. The notaires were about to flee when he relented.

He is nevertheless cherished in the profession for his yarns about his paysans, at once naive and suspicious, generous and stingy. There was the village priest who, when the collection plate kept coming back nearly empty, persuaded his flock to reserve seats in Paradise in advance, at 10 francs a seat! There was the old woman who decided to make a pot au feu for her dying husband, and sent a neighbor to the village for a bit of beef. He returned and said: "Don't you think it would be a waste to give old Guste a stew? He wouldn't even taste it—so I bought him four planks instead." (The planks, of course, were for a coffin.) There was the old notaire who prided himself that he had never had to strike out a word in a document. Taking inventory on a farm one day, his sight failing, he dictated to his clerk: ". . . one red mare, 5 years old, value 1,000 francs." Loud titters from witnesses. The notaire peers under the horse and resumes: "Parenthesis, I say, a mare of male sex, and I specify that this animal is entire. . . ."

Some of Maître Favier's own exploits have entered folk legend as well. Most of them involve tiffs with wardens, policemen, judges, and functionaries of the railroad and the notariat. He explained, "It's the old spirit of the Frenchman, when he'd make a revolution *pour un oui ou pour un non* (at the drop of a beret, so to speak). If he still had it, the technocrats wouldn't put over the tenth part of what they make him swallow now. We are the most downtrodden people in the world."

He didn't look very downtrodden.

["There'll be one more generation of notaires, and then we'll be gone," said Maître Favier. "Who will lose? The client. Now, he goes to someone he likes, who talks over his little affairs. I won't say we help him cheat, but *enfin*, we tell him what he can do, and not to exaggerate. . . . The day it's all bureaucratized, there will be a horde of clerks, and it will cost the state dear. . . . We keep the family papers of France. When we go, it will be the death of the family."]

For centuries, French sovereigns, revolutionaries, and solid bourgeois ministers have threatened to lay hands on this extraordinary institution and its huge resources. In vain. But today, the notariat is in a crisis that many regard as terminal—a crisis reflected in the alarming frequency of arrests of notaires and, wonder of wonders, a strike that closed some 2000 rural *études* for two days this winter. The enormity of such an action may be indicated by the fact that when the bicycle craze swept France in the 1890s, it took grave debates in Chambres des Notaires to rule that a member would not disgrace the profession if he were seen in public on two wheels.

Menaced as it is, the notariat is so deeply entrenched in the French way of life that people are astonished to hear that nothing like it exists in the United States. How, they ask, do you arrange a marriage contract, buy a house, or settle an estate? The American notary public is, to be sure, a vestige of an institution that goes back to the scribes of Babylon, and no doubt beyond. But it is only in the countries of Latin law that deeds and wills must be authenticated by a licensed professional. And among them, France is almost unique in preserving the "venality of the trust," a legal term meaning that the post is owned by its occupant, who may sell it or pass it on to his heirs. The venality of church offices and military commands has long since disappeared, but the word remains a synonym for corruption and for the contested privilege of the French notaire.

It is quite a prize. Through their monopoly on wills and property transactions, all the wealth of France passes through the hands of her 6327 notaires at least once in every lifetime. The notaire is the custodian of an estate until it is distributed among the heirs, which often runs to a year or more. (Maître Favier says Lazarus should be the patron saint of the notaires, because he died twice. Actually, the notaires have two patron saints, Nicholas and Ives; an ancient mock rosary says, "St. Ives was a Breton, a lawyer, and not a thief—a thing of wonder to the people.") In sales of real estate, the notaire holds the payment for a month or so until he clears the title—which he personally guarantees. Maître Emmanuel Villedieu of La Cambe in Normandy, who is the president of the notaires's union, says real estate deals now run to about $30-billion a year, of which the notaires' fees, fixed by law, run to only 1.4 percent. A check of typical deals by other notaires suggested an average take of about twice that.

The marriage contract is a loss leader, at a fee of about $6. Anyway, the negotiation of the material terms of matrimony is no longer what it used to be. "In the old days," said Maître Favier mournfully, "marriages were arranged by families, and they haggled over every clause and every sheet and pillowcase. Now, young people don't give a damn for their parents' opinions. They come in for a contract as if they were buying a packet of chewing gum."

In fact, notaires say, 95 percent of marriages have been consecrated without benefit of contract since 1966, when the law was amended to provide that in such a case joint ownership would apply only to property acquired after the wedding. Before that, the Napoleonic Code called for the community of all property except land. This worked well when most property *was* land, said Maître Claude Brocard of Pont-Sainte Maxence, in Picardy. In those days he recalled, folk wisdom said "movable things are vile things." But when ownership of businesses and securities became more important, marriage without a contract could spell trouble. "I've seen a wedding where the bride was killed in an automobile accident and the groom had to surrender half his fortune to her family," Maître Brocard said.

Despite the 1966 law, many couples still sign contracts as a status symbol or for sound economic reasons: because allowances under a marriage contract are exempt from inheritance tax, and the wife of a bankrupt businessman may,

under the regime of separation of goods, continue to buy and sell. "I had a couple in here once," Maître Favier recalled, "and I asked them what was their matrimonial regime. He looked at his wife kind of funny, and there was a pause. Then she shrugged and said, 'Three times a week.'"

Speaking of the separation of goods in marriage, the Provençal author Marcel Pagnol once wrote, "There are no pockets in a nightshirt." But Maître Favier, also a Provençal, objected, "The main thing is to foresee that a marriage can go sour." The observation, so foreign to Nordic romanticism and optimism, was pure French, as in the typical exchange on a lovely day: "Not bad. . . ." "Mmm . . . provided it lasts."

Realism is the hallmark of another quintessentially French creation of the notaire, the *rente viagère*. In the typical case, a person past middle age and lacking other means sells his home for a lifetime annuity (a *viager*), but continues to occupy his property until his death, when the transfer is made. For the seller, it is a means of obtaining income (a *rente*) while holding on to the homestead—and often it is also a device for disinheriting one's kinfolk. For the buyer, it is a way of acquiring property without a large outlay of capital—provided the seller does not live too long.

Thereon rests a considerable folklore. There is the story of the seller who enters the notaire's study bowed with age, coughing, and at death's door, but revives wonderfully as soon as the contract is signed. A temperance story in a children's textbook tells of a buyer who plies the seller with brandy until the poor chap dies. Life imitates art; not 100 yards from the Place St. Michel in Paris is a valuable house that was sold in viager by its owner, a man so miserly that he ate like a sparrow. The buyers, two neighborhood merchants, insisted on celebrating the deal with a copious repast in one of the best restaurants of the quarter, not sparing the wine. They also set up an apéritif every time the seller came by. He died four weeks later; his heirs contested the transfer but, as an old saying has it, "The notaire has gone over it, it cannot be gainsaid."

Maître Brocard, who arranges ten annuity deals a year, says folklore exaggerated the gruesome aspect of the annuity sale. "It's a straight economic deal," he said. "I have never seen a seller upset by the constant references to his death in the reading of the contract." Maître Favier agreed, with a reservation. Alluding, perhaps, to a movie comedy (*Le Viager*) that is regaling French audiences these days, he observed: "I've never heard of a murder over a *rente viagère*—it would have to be the perfect crime. But I don't deny that buyers are unhappy if the seller lives too long. Ah, there are plenty who don't hide it! I had a first cousin of my mother's once, a middle-aged teacher, who sold a property in viager to a neighbor. He lived to be 90. Every time the neighbor saw my father, he'd say in our language, in Provençal, 'That cousin of yours, he'll never croak.' And my father, when he wanted to annoy this guy, he'd say, 'I just saw my cousin. He's in great shape.' This went on for 40 years."

The notaire's job is to bring buyer and seller together and negotiate the terms, often including a "bouquet" or down payment and a rente based on the value of the property divided by the life expectancy of the seller, as computed in a standard actuarial table.

"One day," Maître Favier recalls, "an old couple came in here and asked me when they were going to die.

"'I don't perform miracles,' says I.

"'But you told our cousin Untel,' says the wife. 'You had it written in a book by the telephone.'"

"And here it is," said Maître Favier, holding up a worn volume of actuarial tables. "Untel had come to me to deed his farm to his kinfolk, a fictitious sale so as to avoid the inheritance tax. I warned him that he might find himself despoiled

47

one day, and suggested that he sell the place in viager instead. To figure the rente, I looked up his life expectancy. And sure enough, he died the year the book said he should. . . . I explained that to the old couple, but they wouldn't believe me. Now, I hide the book."

Even the Finance Ministry cannot say exactly how many rente viagères there are, but it is estimated that there are more than a million. Notaires say that the practice is, like the marriage contract, gradually giving way to the heightened

tempo of modern times; fewer people care to wait for death to close a deal. ("Besides," said a notaire from Savillac, "people live too long nowadays.") But they report this without regret, for the loss in fees from viagers is far more than made up by the boom in real estate transactions of all kinds: subdivisions, building projects, apartment sales, and the rest. The bulk of notarial income is made up by fees from these deals and from their ancillary role as mortgage broker, bringing private lenders together with private borrowers. These are the source of their wealth and, more and more often these days, the cause of their downfall.

By law, notaires are forbidden to invest their own money in transactions they handle, or to make "blind" investments of funds in their custody— that is, where the borrower is unknown to the lender. In practice, the temptation has proved too strong for many of them. Hardly a month goes by without news of the bankruptcy of an étude and the arrest of its owner; when I visited Villeneuve-sur-Lot last winter, two of the town's three *notarial études* had been closed under scandalous circumstances.

In the old days, the *krach* (crash, collapse) of a notaire was extremely rare. Occasionally, one would pull the *coup de la danseuse* and run off with a light lady and the clients' funds (a man in a play by Jean Giraudoux is said to be "living as high as a fugitive notaire"). But the typical case nowadays resembles the 1966 crash of Six-Fours-la-Plage, near Toulon. One out of three notarial scandals is situated on the booming Côte d'Azur; this one was outstanding only because of the sum involved: $7.5 million. Some 1500 small investors of the region had entrusted this sum to Maître Paul Boyancé on his promise to pay interest at 10 percent with no need to trouble the tax collector about it. He in turn lent the money to real estate promoters. When a big project went sour, he dipped into remaining capital to pay the interest, until that was gone, and the gendarmes came. A clamor arose from 1500 voters, and the echo reached the National Assembly. Hastily, the Chambre des Notaires in Paris announced that everybody would be paid promptly and in full. The affair wiped out the reserves of the profession's Collective Guaranty Fund, and a forced levy was imposed on every notary in France.

Dozens of similar scandals in recent years have damaged the image of the notariat. Alain Brocard, a law student, says his classmates now call him "the swindler's son." This is bitter medicine for his father, Maître Claude, who recalls that when he bought his first étude in a village near the Loire, the front pew in church went with it. "I was 26 years old," he said, "and the first Sunday when I went to mass the old peasants made way, and let me know I had to sit in the notaire's place." After a pause, he declared that the public trust was still merited by the 6000 notaires who were "absolutely straight," while being betrayed by "two or three hundred who are absolutely criminal."

But the black sheep have now become a flock, it is said. To be sure, the notariat is collectively responsible for all funds properly in its custody. There, however, is the rub. Maître Brocard, who was taxed $2,000 for the Six-Fours caper, objects bitterly to having been forced to repay people who gave money to a notary for blind investment, in violation of the law, in order to evade taxes.

It should perhaps be noted here that the Frenchman's loathing for the tax collector has a sound historic justification, dating back to the age when the lord claimed first rights to everything from the grain on the peasant's threshing floor and the eggs in his henhouse to the virginity of his bride. (The *droit du seigneur* was often acquitted by a wedding gift to the lord of produce or money.) The *seigneur* was

eliminated by the Revolution, but even bourgeois governments must live, and the cat-and-mouse game of concealment and discovery has gone on ever since. Many old houses are blind because there used to be a tax on windows, and although a peasant no longer hides when he kills a pig, he still prefers high stone walls around the homestead—and still prefers to do business with a close-mouthed notaire.

By the same token, governments since royal times have wanted to take over the notariat. Only Robespierre was tough enough to do it, while he lasted, which insofar as the notaires were concerned was three years. The others have all pulled back before the political and financial power of the notariat—and the enormous indemnity it would take to buy them out. Still, a

prestigious state commission headed by Jacques Rueff and Louis Armand suggested a decade ago that the Government consider paying the price, because the notaires' grip on the supply of capital was holding down economic expansion. Since then, there have been all these scandals, and that explains the haste of the Chambre des Notaires in paying off victims whether innocent or not.

Several country notaires offered the same explanation: the city notaires want at all cost to "drown the fish" (i.e., make no waves), considering that the less said about the profession in the press and in the National Assembly, the better. For the same reason, the city notaires are allegedly hostile to the clamor of their country cousins for an increase in fees, which are set by law. This was a major demand of the 2000 country notaires who struck in December, to the pursed-mouth disapproval of the ruling chambers of the profession. Another demand is more significant. It calls for repeal of a recent decree by the Ministry of Justice, permitting notaires' clerks to substitute for their masters in authenticating deeds.

This horrifies old-fashioned country notaires like Maître Favier, who said, "It will end with the notaire being found quite superfluous." But the decree only legalized a practice already prevailing in some big-city études with scores of clerks, handling many thousands of documents. A majority of papers signed in Paris were null because the notaire could not possibly be present, said an officer of the Syndicat National des Notaires. This is a union formed basically to protect the interest of the country notaires. They form a majority of the Chambres des Notaires, but, as one of them admitted, "We have an inferiority complex toward the city notaires; they're higher born than we are, richer, better educated, closer to the powers that be." Another said, "When they adopt a law, it's these *messieurs de Paris* who are consulted on it."

A country notaire is a general practitioner who, if he has the misfortune to be situated in a depressed area, may actually be quite poor. Some would actually welcome nationalization, with a government salary or pension, though none dares to say so publicly. The more typical specimen is a prosperous and conservative small-town notable, defending a way of life he fears is doomed.

"The priest is going, the doctor is going," said Maître Favier. "Now the notaire is going—practically the only man left to whom one still tips the hat. In the country, that is. In the city, nobody'd recognize a notaire if he saw one."

CORSICA: IN THE SHADOW OF BONAPARTE

Bastia—March, 1967

A little honest election fraud is built into the Corsican system, a citizen explained smilingly over a pastis on the Grand Plaza overlooking the harbor. For one thing, a great many Corsicans are absentees. The 1965 census gave the island a population of 244,000, but it is believed that no more than 150,000 actually live here. The rest, and their children and cousins, are mostly in Continental France, where they are prominent in business, medicine, education, politics, the customs service, the police—and organized crime. "We have some of the best-educated gangsters in the world," the citizen said, seriously.

"The people at home are poor," he went on, "and they depend on their mayors. So the children on the continent vote. That makes the doctors over there politically important. They write the letters saying the voters are sick and the

52

application goes to the mayor. If he needs to, he puts on the names of people who are dead, too. At election time, the people enjoy going to the village hall and seeing all those old names still up there on the lists. Nothing much to be done about it— you'd have to convict all the mayors."

Across the green terraces the two churches still confront each other, no longer hostile, merely redundant. This Easter Sunday, the Latin Church stands deserted (it had its turn last year), while the village is gathered at the Greek Church. As the women follow the Byzantine mass under the liquid eyes of a dozen ikons, the men in Sunday finery chat beside the door, overlooking the blue sea. Small boys keep up a rugged fusillade of firecrackers, which punctuates the ancient Greek chants from the church. Finally, the bearded young priest in his gold-trimmed white robe emerges with his retinue bearing crossed candles. Young men in double file flanking the door fire a salute from their shotguns, and the procession winds its way to the fountain at the top of the village, where the priest blesses the terraced fields.

In his presbytery later, the Reverend Florent Marchiano explained, "The men waiting outside feel they've participated in the mass. It's the Oriental spirit: the parish delegates the priest to pray for them."

Father Florent, as he is called, is possibly unique in the Roman Catholic church, being the priest of two congregations occupying the same parish, one of the Latin, the other of the Eastern rite. Cargèse is pretty unusual, too. It was founded by Greeks fleeing Turkish oppression three centuries ago. In exchange for their haven here, they left what Father Florent calls the schismatic Orthodoxy and recognized the supremacy of the Pope, while preserving their ancient ritual. As farmers and fishermen, they prospered but relations with their Corsican mountaineer neighbors were troubled. When the Corsicans rose first against the Genoans and then against the French, the Greeks sided with their patrons. The last uprising subsided about 1830, but a certain separation remained, symbolized by the two churches.

"Before I came," Father Florent said, "there was a little acrimony. Each priest preached for his own shop. People would play one off against the other. A child who was scolded at catechism would skip the next session and tell his priest later that he'd been across the way. It was his way of getting even."

The Greek church's best singer, 74-year-old Joseph Dappello, came over long ago following a dispute with the Latin priest about the harmonium. On the other hand, the Papadacci family, formerly Papadakis, is now Latin. A Papadacci woman explained cheerfully, "My granduncle was a domineering man, and he thought he would have more influence if he were in the Latin church, so he became a renegade."

The word renegade no longer carries a sting. Over the years, the Greek culture gave way— there are only three old people left who speak the language—and both churches lost ground. On an ordinary Sunday, only about 50 people attend mass in each church, of a population that Father Florent put at 800 year-round, 6000 in vacation time, and something between at elections—this being Corsica. "As everywhere," he said, "there has been a drop in the faith. The young no longer come. Most of them go away. There is nothing here for them, not even a movie. For high school, they must go to Ajaccio, and for university, they must say au revoir to Corsica. There are no jobs, either, except in tourism. Being a bartender is no solution. All this hotel building has its good side—because the village is not, after all, dying—but all you see is new masonry." When the last priests retired eight years ago, the parish could no longer maintain two curates. So Rome found a replacement in Calabria, Italy, where there is an Albanian colony which, like the Greeks of Cargèse, had fled the Turks and preserved the Eastern rite.

Fortunately, Father Florent, then 25, was not married. The ordaining of married men is permitted by the Eastern rite, but might have shocked some Latin parishioners.

"Now," Father Florent said with a smile, "I say mass twice every Sunday, first in one church, then in the other. I switch costumes, I turn my coat, I change my visage. Over there, I become a Latin with the Latins. I baptize here by total immersion. There, I sprinkle. This Easter, I'm blessing houses in Greek, next year it will be in Latin." As for the gunfire that marked the end of the mass, he explained, "It's an Oriental way of expressing joy—Christ is risen!"

The guns sometimes speak more grimly. A fortnight ago, Father Florent followed the gendarmes into a house here where a deranged young man had killed his parents and then himself. Talk of the tragedy turned faces grave in the village cafés beside the little square where children crowded around the Rat Game, a kind of roulette where players guess which hole the white rat will enter. At Nono's café, a law official on a visit home from Ajaccio confided over his pastis

that he was now handling 14 homicide cases, which he thought must be a record.

"Corsica is an unhappy country," he said. "In the past, there was no justice—people made their own. There is our historic custom of bearing arms. Every teenager gets a gun from his father. Crimes here are just like on the mainland, only more stupid. The Corsican is not base, but he has a slightly exacerbated sense of honor. The true Corsican affair begins with an argument, maybe a donkey that has strayed into a neighbor's garden. 'Can't you keep your beast home?' Words pass back and forth, then bang! I had a man in my office who'd shot a guy for making noise by his house. He said, 'What, I can't kill a man under my own window?'"

The talk was more cheerful that evening at the home of Sauveur Rossi, a farmer who had invited some homecoming friends to eat a roast pig, eked out with the famous hard sausage and broccio, or sheep cheese of the country. A straw-covered jug of red wine was emptied, to the toast of "pace et salute" (peace and health). The men recalled some of the village's more colorful characters, like Cecho-echo-echo, who stuttered backwards, repeating final syllables, so that when he tried to pronounce his first name he would say Francecho-echo-echo. There was Bugarone, who at age 104 was so jealous of his womenfolk that he spread sand under their windows, to catch the footprints of any intruders. There was also Ziu (uncle) Loli, who at 90 could still crack snails with his teeth, and who, when electricity came in about 15 years ago, tried to blow out the light. Mr. Rossi, who was an adolescent then, said the boys watched the power lines when the electricity was turned on, and were disappointed when the birds did not fall dead.

Now, electricity has reached into the mountains, and the last chestnut mill of the region, in the hamlet of Renno, is motor driven. Mrs. Paul Susini, the miller's wife, pressed a chestnut doughnut on a woman visitor, saying "Dona grassa, par bella passa," which may be roughly translated as "Fat is beautiful." The Susinis also raise chestnut-fattened pigs and cut some timber. "The mill works only two days a year," she said, "because there's nobody left to gather chestnuts but us. The old die, and the young go away."

Her bachelor brother-in-law, Toussaint Susini, happily greeted visitors to his stone house at Paomia, an all but deserted hamlet on a mountaintop that was the original site of the Greek colony of Cargèse, four miles away as the crow flies, nearly 20 miles by highway and dirt road. From his doorstep, the green slopes swept in weed-grown terraces down to a magnificent expanse of sea. No, he said, there was hardly anybody left; the terraces were too narrow for tractors, the last work oxen vanished some 15 years ago, and who would bring them back? But it was beautiful, and he stayed on.

Nearer town, an old mountaineer weeding a tiny vineyard said grumpily, "No, I didn't march in the Easter procession. When I want to amuse myself, I take my gun into the maquis. There, God can see me. After all, He was born in a stable, wasn't he? Now the priests live in fine houses, but He, He didn't have a house."

Ajaccio—April, 1967

Besides being the birthplace of Napoleon, Ajaccio is probably the only place in the world that has a pig in a stained-glass window. This may be denied —and in fact, since it is a modern abstract stained-glass window it would be difficult to prove—but the story is well known to habitués of Serafina's place, the Restaurant Côte d'Azur on the Cours Napoleon.

A dozen years ago, a country cousin brought a newborn sanglier, or wild piglet, to the patronne, Mrs. Serafina Benedetti. Sanglier is a prized item on the menu, but Ulysses wept, and Serafina surrendered. The pig became the house pet, fed by clients and responding to caresses like a puppy, except that he had hardly any tail to wag. One of the clients was an artist who was doing the windows for the Eglise St. Roch, and he immortalized Ulysses, though it must be acknowledged that in glass he looks more like a green dog. As for the pig himself, he proved all too mortal. One day he slipped out and dug up the garden of the prefecture, and the prefect said he had to go. He went back to the country cousin where. . . Serafina sighs and falls silent.

There are Corsicans still alive who remember when bread was rich people's food, and the common folk lived on chestnuts. Every village had its mill where roasted nuts were ground into flour, which was baked into loaves, or a kind of polenta (like southern cornbread) or doughnuts or gnocchi. Then chestnuts found a market and became dearer than bread, for a time. People's tastes changed, most of the mills were abandoned, and now those chestnuts that are not exported are left on the ground for the pigs, tame or wild. Chestnut cakes have vanished from the market. But Serafina will, on order, fix them for gourmets who can afford them. They are food for the rich, now. Thorstein Veblen, who once wrote how the peasant's clearing became the rich man's lawn, would have found food for thought here.

Corsicans are naturally proud of Napoleon. A pouting portrait of the little emperor is to be seen everywhere. As long as people can remember, Ajaccio (pronounced AH-ZHOX-EE-O) has been run by the Bonapartist party; at election time, the matrons dress in mauve, the emperor's color, and the men parade in mauve sashes. "If you want to succeed," Serafina says, "you must register Bonapartist when very young."

Napoleon is an embarrassing hero, however, to Corsican nationalists—or regionalists, as they prefer to call themselves. His father served the French at a time when they were fighting the patriotic army of Pascal Paoli, the Corsican Washington. Napoleon's birth, in 1769, immediately followed the crushing of Paoli's forces at Pont Novo—which is why Napoleon was born a French citizen rather than a Corsican. Now, the authorities are talking of holding a double celebration in 1969, the two-hundredth anniversary of Napoleon and of Corsica's integration with France. Regionalists like Dominique Alfonsi, the young editor of *La Corse*, say that if the powers insist on celebrating the annihilation of Corsican patriots, there are likely to be "incidents." Incidents in Corsica tend to be fairly dramatic. Mr. Alfonsi, for example, dismissed a recent flare-up of peasants as "nothing at all—just a few bombings."

Mr. Alfonsi is himself a moderate who concedes that, on balance, French rule has been beneficial. Another young intellectual in Serafina's retorted, "What has France ever done for Corsica? Nothing."

A visitor observed that the cigarettes the intellectual was chainsmoking were tax free, and so one-third cheaper than on the continent. "Yes," he replied, "liquor, cigarettes . . . all the things that are bad for us."

The regionalists are in general young university graduates who say they want to turn the clock forward, not back. They want a greater degree of autonomy that would end the dependence of Corsica on Paris, which they say helps account for the crookedness of local politics. The villages receive subsidies on the basis of population, so it is to their advantage to keep the election lists padded with the dead and the absent. Political life is dominated by the clan, partly tribal, partly social. "A man seeks protection and favors through the clan," Mr. Alfonsi said. In local elections, the clans have tended to vote for the moderate left, but nationally they have voted with whatever regime was in power.

"All underdeveloped regions vote for the administration," a diner observed. "Brittany, Guadeloupe, Martinique . . ."

But Senator François Giacobbi, himself a clan leader and chief of the left forces which were counted out of the recent elections here, offered a bitter comment. "Corsica," he said, "is always one election behind. It voted for the administration when it was going under."

Sartène—August, 1969

It was the hour of the apéritif, which in fact took up most of the long summer day. Under the trees of the Place Porta small elderly men in somber jackets and wide-brimmed felt hats gazed impassively at the younger Corsicans from the mainland, the women in tight slacks and the men in easy sportswear. The square is a triangle formed by the church, a few stores, and a café terrace. Actually there are three cafés, and only the dogs playing follow-the-leader among the tables seem unaware of the invisible barriers that separate them.

"Professionally and politically," said an editor from Paris, "I belong at the Bien Assis. But because of my family I have to sit at the Victoire."

The Bien Assis (which might be translated as Sitting Pretty) is the "in" café for the new professional class, most of its members now home for their annual visits. The adjoining Victoire, called "the Communist café," was the headquarters of the wartime resistance and is now the social-political powerhouse of Sartène. A third establishment, the Café des Amis, was a bit apart, shabby, and nearly deserted. Once it was the proudest of all.

"It used to be practically a private club of landowners," said a shopkeeper at the Bien Assis. "Back before the Great War, a carpenter went in there and they tried to throw him out. A man was killed, and the carpenter had to take to the maquis." The landowners are often poor now, and powerless, but the rancor lingers.

"A man can rise to be a prefect," the shopkeeper said, "but if his grandfather was a goatherd, they regard him as a goatherd."

This drew a smile of agreement from a handsome, swarthy man who looked like an Italian peasant but was actually a French diplomat. Encouraged, the shopkeeper went on, "Don ——— di ——— once, for a wonder, gave a serf a lift in his carriage during a rainstorm. After going a little way he became aware that the serf stank, so he told him to get down, saying, 'You know, the happiness of the poor never lasts long.'"

A stranger had asked about the slogan at the portal, calling Sartène "the most Corsican of Corsican towns." The editor, shrugging, pointed out that the capital, Ajaccio, 50 miles of hairpin road to the north, boasts of being the birthplace of Napoleon, and that Propriano, on the coast six miles to the west, daringly advertises itself as "the Corsican St. Tropez." So Sartène, he explained, having neither Bonaparte nor beach, brags about its authenticity. A gray stone town of 6000, it is perched for safety on the shoulders of a mountain, well inland. The relatively fertile coastal lowlands and the fishing grounds were long shunned because of Moorish raids and the malarial mosquito. During World War II the American liberators, using DDT, eradicated the mosquito and, it is said, most of the wild life.

A siren blew, a little fire engine came to the square, half a dozen young men with chrome helmets leaped aboard and it roared off. Several times a day in this rainless summer, fire breaks out in the maquis, the fragrant, green-brown brush that covers the rugged hills. The maquis, which has given its name to the guerrilla, is hospitable only to goats and hunted men. For many centuries, it supported, after a fashion, hundreds of "bergers," or herders, virtual serfs who eked out what their herds earned with little patches of grain and vines. One of the last of the bergeries still occupied was typical: a low, tile-roofed stone hut without a chimney, with a small cooking fire burning in an open hearth in the middle, charring the beams and smoking the goat cheeses and pork hanging overhead.

Little wonder, said the diplomat, that the bergers found the army a better life than at home and that their sons deserted the maquis for the colonies or the mainland. Now the town lives largely on pensions and remittances from some in the professions and government service. Some have also made careers in the underworld. A stranger was shown one of the best houses in town and told, "It's been empty for five years and will be empty for seven more." It was a delicate way of saying that the owner was doing 12 years. It would not do to be more blunt, for Corsica's

harsh past has nurtured a tradition of family solidarity and of class and clan warfare that is far from extinct.

"Oh, it was a perpetual fusillade," said a handsome blonde Parisienne.

"Only 20 years ago," the editor recalled, "boys and girls walked separately here. There were still serenades under the balcony, with guitars, and the little girls would run messages. But if a boy and girl were seen together, the girl's father, or older brother, would call on the boy's family. A marriage would follow, or else"—he pointed his hand like a pistol—"ping!"

The last paroxysm of violence in Corsica came during the war, when the Italians occupied the island, which had been under Roman and Italian rule for long stretches of its history. "The landowners," the shopkeeper said, "collaborated with the Genoese in olden times, then with the French, and then with the Italians. During the resistance the sons of the serfs took their vengeance." Afterward the Communists took over the Town Hall. They still hold it, with Socialist support, and the diplomat said they had given Sartène its first effective and modern administration.

As for the aristocrats, he went on, they have fallen on hard times. The maquis having been abandoned by the shepherds, they have sold what arable land there is to emigré Europeans from Algeria, who are tilling it with Arab workmen. The storekeeper smilingly recalled the reply of a needy aristocrat to an offer of a job: "A Pietri does not work."

"You remember Tante Maria-Tonietta?" the storekeeper asked. "She heard the kids chanting by the church. 'God help the poor, because the rich don't need it.' She told them not to say that any more. She said they should chant, 'Help the rich, because the poor can earn their own living.'"

"Ah," the storekeeper concluded, "the young people are sweeping all that away."

Part Three **LA FOIRE**

THE PARDON OF THE NEWFOUNDLANDERS

The Pardon des Terre Neuvas, the rite that for centuries has marked the departure of Norman fishermen for the Newfoundland banks, has foundered in a sea of bitterness. The fleet owners blame the fishermen's union, the union blames the owners, and both blame the Common Market. The clergy, distressed, has strong words for the Government.

According to tradition, men from Fécamp were crossing the Atlantic in search of cod before Columbus. At any rate, nobody seems to know when the Pardon, also known as St. Peter of the Sailors, began. But on the Sunday before the fleet set sail, children would receive first communion, in dead of winter instead of in May, so that their fathers could be present. There would be a Mass for the dead, a general remission of sins for those who would not return, a procession bearing model boats from the Gothic church of St. Etienne to the harbor, and a blessing of the sea and the boats. The day became known by the name of the patron saint of the fishermen, St. Peter of the Sailors, or as the Pardon of the Newfoundlanders, the name applied both to the men and to their vessels.

The rite was suspended during the war, along with the "grande peche," or codfishing. Afterward, a local booster picked it up. The navy was brought in, politicians came from Paris, the Cardinal came from Rouen, and tourists came from everywhere. To accommodate the throng, the high Mass was moved three years ago from St. Etienne, the fishermen's parish, to the Benedictine Abbey, which is about the size of St. Patrick's Cathedral. The fishermen stayed in their parish.

"It was no longer St. Peter of the Sailors," said Francis St. Cast. "It was St. Peter of the Owners."

Mr. St. Cast, who is 30 years old and has been a fisherman since he was 13, is ship's delegate of the *Viking*, the largest and newest trawler-freezer plant in the Fécamp fleet. The *Viking* was to have sailed January 10, three weeks before the older vessels, but its crew refused to go aboard without a guaranteed price for cod. The crew of the trawler is paid one-fifth of the catch, minus the cost of food. Last fall, while the fleet was at sea, the price of cod fell and the take was less than expected. A typical fisherman earned about $1,350 for the year. That, Mr. St. Cast told an interviewer, is for ten months at sea, working 12 hours on and 6 hours off when the fish are running. "Off Labrador," he said, "I've seen it ten below, and nets to be mended."

Someone observed that it was not very gay for the men, nor for the wives at home, and wondered why they stayed with it.

"You must understand," Mr. St. Cast said earnestly, "this trade is carried in the blood, from father to son. A woman who marries a seaman, well, she knows what awaits her."

To press its case while government officials were on hand, the Communist-led union called a demonstration in the port. Thereupon Jean York, one of the owners of the *Viking* and chairman of the sponsoring committee, canceled the Pardon. He said he did not want it to be "used" politically.

The owners finally granted the fishermen a price guarantee, and the crew of the *Viking*, reluctantly abandoning other demands, agreed to sail. It was too late, however, to revive the procession, the banquets, and the naval visit.

There was a high mass in the church of St. Etienne, which was decked in fishnets, lifebuoys, and ensigns, and filled by townsfolk, political notables, the city band, boat owners and captains, but hardly any fishermen. The Most Reverend André Pailler, Archbishop of Rouen, said in a sermon that the maritime world was facing a crisis that menaced its survival. "You are few," he declared, "and hence you risk being overlooked in the time of great choices."

The Archbishop was alluding to a fear expressed by many here, that the Government would neglect the fishing industry in order to save more vital interests, in Common Market negotiations. The great complaint of the industry has been that competing foreign fleets, especially those of West Germany, enjoy subsidies denied to French fishermen. This is blamed for the drop in fish prices. A Common Market agreement to equalize conditions of competition in fishing has long been proposed but is far from adoption. If the Government decides that it cannot save the fishing industry, the Archbishop said, "the people should be warned honestly, in time to prepare them for a reconversion."

In a nearby café, Jacques Ledun, an elderly owner, said he thought the Archbishop might have overstated the crisis.

"The cod," he said, "is still profitable, with a little will. You can make money if you want to work. The trouble here has been all political. The fisherman is rather susceptible to promises. More leisure time? You can't put a rugby field on a trawler."

Mr. Ledun said he thought the Pardon might survive, in the form of an annual high Mass. But the rite of the old Newfoundlanders, about to sail into the lonely North Atlantic, appears to have ended forever. The sponsors have decided to stage the event in August, when a maximum of tourists can be on hand. And a minimum of fishermen.

THE TRUFFLE MARKET

Nature and women in their mysterious ways have endowed this poor region of Southwest France with two maladies of rich price: the subterranean fungus known as the truffle and the distended liver of overfed birds. The appropriate tone in talking about them is one of profound gloom. As every peasant knows, it is bad luck to mention good fortune, and would only attract envy. Not to mention the tax collector. This makes selling truffles in the public market a rather unusual proceeding.

The buyers, a clump of stocky men, loiter under the trees beyond the goose market. Each wears a leather money pouch and carries an iron hand scale, whose name, *la romaine*, betrays its antiquity. Every now and then, a countryman or a countrywoman will idle by, bearing a basket of eggs, groceries, or a goose—or nothing at all. There is not a truffle in sight. One of the buyers, however, accosts the peasant and asks what he has. After a sharp look at the buyer and at possible witnesses, the peasant delves to the bottom of the basket or into a capacious pocket, and out comes a sack of redolent brown lumps.

The buyer peers at them, and names a price. The seller may protest, haggle, and even depart, to return or seek another buyer. But most often, he just nods and shrugs with resignation. The buyer weighs the truffles, tosses them carelessly into a wicker hamper and counts out the money from a well-filled pouch. The peasant hastily tucks it away and disappears.

Among themselves, the peasants grumble about truffle prices, which average about one dollar an ounce. This is at least 50 cents less than last year, but that reflects a sharp rise in production. The rainy summer and fall, disastrous for the wine, was just dandy for truffles.

"Truffles is not farming, it's luck," said Emile Couderc, a five-foot-tall farmer.

Truffles are, in fact, a mystery that has defied savants at least since Plutarch and Pliny. The black Périgord variety, dear in both senses of the word to gourmets, is found generally in stony, porous soil around the roots of scrub oaks—but only some oaks, and nobody knows why those are chosen. A French peasant is credited with having discovered early in the eighteenth century that acorns from infected oaks, planted in similar soil, may—just may—yield truffles too, in 10 or 15 years. One out of ten truffle-bearers is a good average. Agronomists are still trying to raise the yield by injecting truffle spores among the roots, but this artificial insemination has so far proved sterile.

63

Mr. Couderc agreed with Alain Pébeyre, a white-bearded patriarch who at 84 is still one of the world's leading truffle merchants, that the days of the black mushroom in these parts are numbered. They explained that few peasants nowadays had the capital or the patience to plant diseased oaks and wait ten years to find out whether they had money or firewood. Mr. Couderc said small farming was just about through, what with prices and government policies fluctuating wildly. "Last year they subsidized us to raise cows," he said, "and this year they subsidize us not to." Mr. Pébeyre said with all these corporate mergers, small business was on the way out, too.

He shook his head at the perfidy in the world— pork butchers, for example, who "truffle" their sausages with the cheap black, quite harmless, mushroom called trumpet of death, or merchants who dye black the common, and rather tasteless, white summer truffle. The true Périgord truffle, he said, is a fungus of remarkable qualities aside

from gastronomy. When his workers cut themselves peeling truffles, he said, the cuts never become infected. The ancients were absolutely right, he added, in regarding the truffle as aphrodisiac. He himself seldom ate truffles any more, Mr. Pébeyre said. "When I want a truffled chicken or an omelette," he explained, "I have only to leave the bird or the eggs in the truffle locker overnight."

Mr. Pébeyre said some men could sniff out a truffle unaided, or could find them by watching the female truffle fly boring into the ground to lay her eggs. But peasants generally rely on dogs or pigs. Hereabouts, dogs are unpopular with the peasants. A hunter or a woman pet lover may be walking innocently in the woods with a dog—or they may be trying to bag a truffle or two. "A lady will hardly go strolling with a pig," Mr. Pébeyre explained.

Mr. Couderc, who cautiously acknowledged owning "a few" truffle trees, said training a truffle pig was no problem at all.

"You go to the fair in the spring with a bit of truffle," he explained. "And you offer it to a pig. It's better not to let the owner see it, because the price goes up. Anyhow, if the pig eats it, you buy. "That's all there is to it. You walk him on a rope, he instinctively smells the truffle. Soon he develops a trick. He shoves his snout down on this side, then that side, then he opens his mouth. You pull him back quickly, and give him some corn or a potato."

By the end of the season, the pig is getting too big to be manageable, and he will be eaten the following fall. Hence, Mr. Couderc said, peasants do not give their truffle pigs pet names. But townsfolk sometimes call them Saint Anthonys, after the saint who is often portrayed with a porcine friend.

Buyers in the goose and duck market were as gloomy as the truffle merchants about the future of their business, and for much the same reason. It was a bit difficult to uncover the price situation, because no two dealers would agree on it, but an average indicated that goose liver, selling at about the same price as truffles, was far dearer than last year, with demand almost unlimited. The trouble is, everybody agreed, that young farm wives simply refuse to fatten birds. Fattening is a woman's business. On a typical farm, an old woman will call in her little flock of 10 or 20 birds three times a day, and with a funnel poke mash down their throats, working it down with a milking hand motion. Soon, like well-fed Frenchmen, they develop a liver.

The bird reaches market either whole or in parts. The liver—foie gras—is of course the precious cash crop, destined mainly for Paris and the world market. The natives happily buy up the rest, for confit, or conserve; for friton, a sort of pâté; for rillette, a mincemeat; and for cooking fat. Even the remaining carcass, roasted, is a prized local delicacy, and the blood, sold in dried cakes, is served as pudding.

On special occasions during the season, burghers will treat themselves to a fresh foie gras at La Taverne. Five of them, all 61 years old, were observed the other day at table, in their annual class reunion.

They began with champagne and smoked salmon, followed by foie gras with capers, then a *gratin de langouste* with white burgundy. Clearing the palate with a sherbet doused in calvados, they switched to the local Cahors wine and tackled a boar steak with what Chef Pierre Escorbiac calls exotic rice (with green pepper). They ended with cheese, crêpes suzettes, and some old Armagnac and new pear brandy.

Four hours after they had sat down to table they paused for a parting handshake with the chef, and a few gloomy words about the truffle market. Things were not, they agreed, what they used to be. And they never would be again.

THE SELF-STUFFING GOOSE

Benquet—February, 1972

In the secrecy of their laboratories, scientists of a number of countries are racing to invent the self-stuffing goose. Having already bewitched the goose into mating like people, more or less, they are now getting it to overeat like people. It is a prospect to drool at—foie gras for the masses.

Foie gras is of course a fatty liver, such as Frenchmen tend to pat when they say they are not feeling well. Now the goose is not a barnyard intellectual, but it's too smart to overeat, normally. French peasant women have overcome this reluctance in a traditional way, by pushing grain down the bird's throat, three times a day. After three weeks or so of this—foie gras. Demand for this unctuous gland is such that farm wives were getting nine to ten dollars a pound for

goose liver at market this week, not to mention
the rest of the bird. When a bit of truffle is added
(at about $23 a pound), it makes up a handsome
export item. But France is now able to market
only 800 tons a year, including large amounts
imported from Hungary, Poland, and, recently,
Israel, to be processed into paste at Strasbourg.

Georges Monachon, one of the world's leading
authorities on the goose, thinks France can do
much better. He explained why as he guided a
visitor around the great experimental goose ranch
he directs for the Government here. Hundreds of
birds hissed and honked their disapproval as the
men, clad in antiseptic white coats and plastic
shoe covers, passed by. They can really be quite
affectionate, Mr. Monachon said, and will lay
more eggs for a friendly handler than for one
they don't like. On farms, for the right mistress,
they will come to the barn on call to be stuffed.
But stuffing is a tedious job. It has been eased by
the invention of a screw within the funnel, which
is cranked by hand to push food down, in place of
the old poking stick. Now electric motors are
replacing the crank handle. But it still takes two
and one-half hours of a woman's time, over three
weeks, to complete the stuffing of one goose.

The dazzling possibility of getting the goose to
do it on its own was opened by American research
on the hypothalamus, a sector of the brain that
controls certain senses. A spot in this area called
the center of satiety tells the animal when it has
had enough. When it is damaged, the beast will
eat like a pig. It was on pigs that French
researchers began their studies. Surgeons, then
interested primarily in studying the human brain,
developed the technique of destroying the center
of satiety with an electric needle.

Once recovered from the operation, the beast
ate for three and fattened accordingly. From an
economic point of view, an overfat pig is not
particularly desirable. But the goose is something
else again. The same operation was performed on

several hundred birds from Mr. Monachon's ranch, under the direction of Dr. Pierre Auffray. He reported similar results as with the pig: the birds ate nearly as much as if they were stuffed by hand and yielded decent foie gras, somewhat smaller than the normally abnormal.

Mr. Monachon envisages a mobile surgery that would tour goose farms on a truck, with a trained crew of technicians operating on the hypothalami by the thousands. But Dr. Auffray said in a telephone interview that more work needed to be done.

At best, the operation takes half an hour of skilled labor time, which makes its economic validity questionable. But Dr. Auffray revealed that he was working with an American drug company using a product he was not ready to identify, to stun the center of satiety by injection.

There is a problem of toxicity, to the goose, not the consumer, Dr. Auffray said. If the technique is perfected, he predicted, a bird could be made self-stuffing in a ten-minute operation at negligible cost.

Mr. Monachon indicated that another problem had been largely solved. Goose-stuffing has been highly seasonal because goose procreation is highly seasonal. (This problem is not crucial with ducks, who behave more like people.) But by jiggling the length of the day with artificial lighting, Mr. Monachon and other breeders have managed to confuse geese about the calendar. As a result, fresh foie gras has recently become a year-round item in some Paris restaurants. It also means that goose raising and processing can be year-round trade, and thus more attractive.

An enthusiast of modern farming, Mr. Monachon runs into a lot of resistance in this traditional southwest corner of France. Referring to one critic, he commented: "Why did he sell his oxen for a tractor?"

A skeptical view was expressed by a sturdy peasant, Marcel Castay, the Mayor of Trie-sur-

Baise, after the weekly pig and foie gras market. "They talk lots of theory," he said, "but it's practice that counts when you're stuffing a goose.

They're vaccinating everything, they're getting away from the soil. But the goose is a strong critter. We're not there yet."

THE HOME OF THE BEAN

Arpajon—September, 1971

As they do after every fall harvest, tens of thousands of Frenchmen came to Arpajon to celebrate the green bean known as the flageolet.

That every wine has the taste of the soil where it grew is commonly known. But to the educated French palate, the *gout de terroir*, the taste of the earth, is savored in even the humblest products of the soil, each of which has its predestined region of *grands crus*.

Around market stalls, connoisseurs often dispute whether the best butter comes from Deux-Sèvres or Isigny, the best beef from the Charolais or the Limousin, the best poultry from Bresse, Périgord, or Le Mans. But nobody denies that the best potatoes come from the Île de Ré, the best turnips from Nantes, and the best flageolets from Arpajon.

The flageolet was born here one rainy year in the 1870s, when a peasant named Gabriel Chevrier picked his shell beans early and hung them in a shed to dry, fearing they would rot if left outdoors. They kept a fresh flavor for many months. He selected the best for seed, and developed the chevrier variety, now cherished around the world as the natural companion of a leg of lamb.

The bean fair this year was much like those that have gone before, only bigger—less bean and more fair. The reason was apparent on the train ride down from Paris. Middle-aged Parisians fondly remember the "Little Train from Arpajon" which rolled down the Boulevard St. Michel every night to Les Halles, laden with the produce of the truck farms stretching from the outskirts of the city.

The little train has been gone for many years, and the great iron pavilions of Les Halles are being hauled to the scrapyards, both victims of a certain kind of city growth. And from the windows of the aluminum commuter car, concrete apartment houses and row dwellings can be seen springing up among the surviving truck farms and woods. The suburbs are spreading across the 20 miles to Arpajon. In the town hall, where the notables of the region (in slang, the "gros legumes") gathered, a placard hailed the town's newest real estate project, the Meadow Apartments. French promoters often honor in their titles the châteaus, woods, and farmlands they destroy.

After the first *vin d'honneur*, or ceremonial glass, of the day, the notables formed in

68

procession behind a gendarmerie band and toured the fair, whose stalls line the streets of the old village. As they passed the rides, the shooting galleries, the wheels of chance, the ring-a-duck-and-take-it-home stand, the sausage sellers, the mounds of garlic and onions, the bean sellers, the farm equipment, and the long stretches of cheap furniture and appliances, a matron confided that the country aspect of the fair had all but vanished.

"The truck farmers have sold out to the builders," she explained. "Now we have all kinds of problems—sewage, public facilities. The average age now is less than 20 years, and we can't cope. I'm afraid the whole area is going Communist."

Camille Dijon, mayor of the nearby village of Guibeville, confirmed that the production of flageolets and other produce was rapidly declining in this area, and drifting toward Chartres. A stocky little farmer who raised ten acres of the beans this year, he said the shift was not only due to the suburban sprawl.

"It's above all a question of labor," he said. "It's a very delicate crop—a little rain in late summer and it's stained. Last month, there was hail in Beauce, and 50 percent of the crop was lost. When it rains, we call in the canners." But canned flageolets are not the same; they tend to be mushy. The proper dried chevrier is expensive, about 40 cents a pound here in Arpajon, but incomparable. He added that while the chevrier variety would grow almost anywhere, only this region of Île de France could give it its incomparable flavor. If suburbia takes over, the Arpajon bean will become extinct.

In a corner of the seventeenth-century market shed, where a series of gastronomic contests were being held, two young merchants said they faced the same problem in their own trade. "The young people don't want to make cheese," one said. "The tragedy of our country is production: everybody wants to double his output of hay. So they use chemicals, and they sell the milk to the big plants —which can't work with big amounts the way you do with small."

The display was, however, evidence of a countermovement. The two young men were members of a society of cheese merchants and producers aimed at maintaining a public demand for quality cheeses that would assure a good living to young farmers who preserved the old standards.

There is also a movement in this region to halt the issuance of building permits. The flageolet is not dead yet.

69

A TON OF BLOOD SAUSAGE

Mortagne-au-Perche—March, 1972

Long ago, this Norman village set its annual fair in the middle of Lent, because nobody else was having one then. Not so long ago, the local notables chose the boudin, or blood sausage, as theme of the fair, again because nobody else was doing it. That explains why thousands of Frenchmen stood in a freezing wind on a bleak March Sunday, shouting, "Allez France!" while a score of countrymen stuffed themselves with cold blood sausage. The champion, Michel Huré, ate three pounds, or about two yards, in 15 minutes, and said he'd have done better if someone had refilled the glass of water that was its only accompaniment.

A second contest, the pig steeplechase, was won by an entry named Enrillette, pronounced like Henriette but misspelled in a porcine pun on rillette, a meat paste. The names of the winners

70

of the third and most important competition, for the best boudins in the world, were withheld for a week. This is a normal precaution, taken to protect the judges.

There were 603 entries from seven countries—boudin from France, black pudding from England, blutwurst from Germany—but none from the United States. "What I want to know is," said Bill Whitfield, a pork butcher and loyal Rotarian from Washington, in the North of England, "why don't the Americans come?"

One reason, evidently, is a certain finickiness about blood sausage. This is reflected in *Webster's*, which defines *boudin* as a French word meaning "a kind of entrée prepared with delicate forcemeat." This might correctly describe the boudin blanc, a pale sausage which is, to be sure, served along with the true boudin at Christmas time. Boudin and pudding are, of course, basically the same word, meaning sausage, but Webster traced it to Middle English and even Anglo-Saxon, while the *Dictionnaire* of Robert calls it Ancien Français. There is no reason to quarrel, however, since the Normans may well have carried the word across the channel in either direction and, anyway, neither side invented it.

Larousse Gastronomique says some authorities trace blood sausage back to ancient Babylon. Its universality is doubtless based on a repugnance for waste, as voiced by the legendary cannibal who reproaches the European for not eating the people he kills. Mr. Whitfield explained: "A pork butcher must use all the waste, and thus bring down the price of the wholesome parts, like the hams."

Jack Thornley, a contest judge from Lancashire, added grimly: "When we get into the Common Market, black pudding is all we'll be able to afford."

It costs about 40 American cents a pound in England, he said. Emile Husset, a local pork butcher, put the price of boudin at roughly 65

71

onion to a pale gold, and blend all into a silky black paste, while the English like their diced fat to remain conspicuous. Both regard blutwurst as not true blood sausage, because the Germans use it as a setting for noble cuts such as tongue and ham. On the other hand Max Rinkenburger, a wurst manufacturer from the Black Forest, confided that the boudin seemed to him "a sort of peasant type."

An elderly villager said Mortagne had six charcuteries, or delicatessens, and six kinds of boudin. The secret lies in the seasoning, and none of the charcutiers would reveal his own. Besides spices and herbs, some add a dash of Cognac. In the Limousin, peasants still add chestnut flour, and in other regions raisins are used—both doubtless of ancient origin. *Larousse* lists 16 areas of France whose boudins are highly regarded. Regrettably, Normandy is not among them. When pressed, the Mortagnais acknowledge that, while they have always eaten boudin on Wednesdays in wintertime (because pigs are slaughtered on Monday and sausage is made on Tuesday), their real favorite is *rosbif* (roast beef), although they do not look down their noses at a *poularde à la crême*.

Anyhow, the Boudin Fair has proved a brilliant success, and rival communities throughout the region have paid it the flattery of imitation. Now there are a Tripe Fair, local wine fairs, an Andouillette (tripe sausage) Fair, even a Roast-Leg-of-Lamb Fair. Each has its own solemn rite of initiation into an order like the Chevaliers du Tastevin, popular with American visitors to Burgundy. All the notables of Mortagne (pop. 4708) and all distinguished visitors are Knights of the Boudin-Tasting, entitled to wear the ribbon, porcelain medal, and robes of the order. Watching the mass initiation at the annual banquet this year, a resident remarked, "It began as sort of a joke, but they take it seriously now." He was wearing his own ribbon and medal.

cents a pound. But they are not quite the same. For one thing, the English use large amounts of cereal in their sausage—in fact, a joke about wartime rationing was: "Now we have two kinds of bread: bread and sausages."

The English butchers' condescension toward their own black pudding may also be related to the fact that it is more often than not eaten boiled, for breakfast. "Oh, la! Not in water?" exclaimed Mr. Husset, who was properly grilling boudins over a charcoal fire. Mr. Thornley acknowledged that the French variety was "a little tastier." Aside from the cereal, the basic recipe is the same: roughly equal amounts of onion, fat, and fresh pork blood cooked together. But the French sauté the

72

KNIGHTS OF THE TRIPE

Longny-au-Perche—May, 1970

Despite their top hats, the knights of the Fellowship of the Dish of Tripe are not all snobbish about their favorite food. In fact, their annual award dinner at the village hall began not with tripe, but with mountains of asparagus. These were followed by tripe, to be sure, and then by salmon in crayfish sauce. The *trou Normand*— a pause punctuated by calvados—freshened palates for leg of lamb with white and green shell beans, a salad, cheese, fruit, an omelette norvegienne, and coffee. As might be surmised, the lovers of tripe tend to know the value of a sou, and it was noteworthy that this repast, moistened by apéritifs, wines of Alsace, the Rhône, Bordeaux, and Champagne, and coffee and liqueurs, cost the knights a bit more than $5 each.

It was a generous effort to perpetuate a tradition that needed no ceremony until about 20

73

years ago. In those good old days, Longny was the site of a famous monthly horse market. Farmers and draymen came from all over Europe to bid for percherons, a noble race of huge, gentle animals raised in the rich meadows of the valley of the Perche. By custom, the traders would refresh themselves with hearty dishes of tripe and pitchers of cider, purveyed by the 96 taverns that once adorned this township of 1500 souls. The market is gone, and the tractor and the beer truck have relegated the percheron to the status of a show animal. But on long winter evenings the few surviving taverns still serve tripe on the house to players of coinchéu, a card game related to pinochle. And the May Day weekend, which elsewhere is symbolized by the clenched fist and/or the lily of the valley, is here the occasion for an annual tripe festival.

Its central event is the National Contest for the Best Dish of Tripe, which this year drew 86 entries from six corners of France. The jellied entries were *mises en terrine*, or interred in numbered clay pots, to assure anonymity under the watchful eye of a court bailiff, then heated in the ovens of Daniel Lejeune, grand master of the tripe fellowship, 1968 international champion of blood sausage, and gold medalist in rillette, a pork spread. Mr. Lejeune is a local charcutier, theoretically a pork butcher but actually an artisan of sausages, rillettes, pâtés, and a host of other ready-to-serve foods. In the old days, a charcutier would not sell tripe, which is usually from the stomachs of steers and falls in the domain of tripiers, who specialize in innards. But the homogenization of modern life has brought tripe into the stalls of charcutiers and beef butchers as well.

Behind a railing in a circus tent pitched in the village square, a group of judges circulated among the terrines, a fork in one hand, a glass of cider or white wine in the other. The technique called for stirring the dish to see how closely it achieved the desired appearance: neat squares of tripe, evenly assorted among the several areas of the steer's two stomachs, afloat in a rich but smooth and gleaming broth. Then head down to the surface to test the aroma with a deep sniff. Finally, a good mouthful of tripe for the ultimate test.

It was an open contest, and Mr. Lejeune, a middle-aged man with the figure of a charcutier, observed that many entries were obviously from restaurant chefs—that is, fancied up with spices, mushrooms, beans, even olives.

"A charcutier," he said firmly, "would never do a thing like that. You take some leaf and honeycomb tripes and oxfoot—that's primordial! A guy who makes tripe without it . . ."

He left unfinished this allusion to the calf's-foot heresy, which Escoffier himself has denounced, and he resumed: "You put in some onion, carrot, maybe a bit of tomato, clove, pepper and salt, all bathed in a good white wine, and you cook it slowly, all night. In the morning, I take out the foot bones, eat a dish of tripe, and pour the rest into molds."

"Some of these entries were made with cider," grumbled a judge. "I'm from Paris, and I don't like cider."

Actually, the standard recipe for tripes à la mode de Caen, like its Norman and Breton cousins, calls for cider, doubtless because the north country grows apples and not grapes. But cider tends to blacken tripe, so many cooks prefer wine. And wine was the ingredient in the winning terrine, made by André Moinard, a charcutier in Bayeux, Normandy.

May Day was indeed the charcutiers' day, for it was a 19-year-old professional, Jean-Yves Leroy of Chambord, who won the 15-minute tripe-eating race against nine other contenders, before a crowd of 1000. It was scarcely a contest. Mr. Leroy took the lead from the opening, forking up tripe in a deceptively relaxed style, with an air of evident pleasure. He drew a loud cheer when he

finished his first 2.6-pound terrine, daintily licked his fingers, and signaled for more. In the final minute, observing his glazed competition at a standstill, Mr. Leroy put his fork down and waited for the bell. He had set a new record at 4 pounds, 3 ounces of tripe.

The young charcutier confided that he had rather cut down on lunch before the contest, contenting himself with a salad, veal with salsify and morels, and some cheese. As for his dinner to come, he said he had an open mind on the subject.

The loyalty of this Norman community to tradition drew approval from Jean-Baptiste Even, a Breton schoolteacher who had served as a tripe judge. "In the village of Le Feuillé in Finistère," he observed, "a wedding dinner always begins with tripe, and it's said that if the tripe is good, the marriage will be happy."

FISHING WITH A WRENCH

Rouvray—March, 1970

The custom of harvesting fish on the Monday of Holy Week is fading along with many other village traditions, a victim of progress and pollution. So the biennial work festival here was not to be missed. Time was when thousands of communities would turn out at this season to drain a pond and share the fish. This date was preferred because it was spring, a holiday time, and meat was forbidden until Easter Sunday. Now, the ban on meat has been lifted, and lake fish is less of a treat than it was. In areas of intensive farming, insecticides and defoliants have poisoned many ponds. Elsewhere, a good many owners still take in a crop of carp, pike, tench, and perch every two years, but few of them try to have any fun while doing it.

Here, despite a chilling rain, a score of ruddy Burgundian peasants kept the faith at Vanoise Pond. The work actually had begun on Palm Sunday, when they set up a huge steel crib called a tombereau to catch the fish as they came through the dam gate. Then Jacques Untel, a stout, elderly peasant in a blue smock, cranked the sluice open a few notches to let the pond out, slowly. Half a dozen volunteers took shelter in a nearby shack for the night, fortified with wine, bread, sausage, pâté, and the card game called tarot, to watch the water level and keep poachers away.

Dawn came imperceptibly. The leafless skeletons of poplar trees dripped on spreading mud flats, and upstream two ducks flapped up from reeds, circled the shrinking pond, and flew off. A dozen men wearing hip boots arrived in cars and on tractors and climbed into the tombereau. Mr. Untel cranked the sluice gate wide open and a torrent rushed into the crib, bearing mud, leaves, twigs, and fish. While some of the men swung twig brooms and pitchforks to clear the trash, others seized squirming fish and heaved them into boxes, which were carried off by a moving chain of volunteers to be sorted, weighed, and put in freshwater tanks.

Villagers lined the bank, swapping shouted insults with the workmen and waiting their turn to buy fish. From time to time, the men shouted to the gate tender to slow the stream, or to speed it up. At midmorning, Mr. Untel was cranking when the handle slipped loose and fell into the mud—lost forever. He looked down, then reached deep into his vocabulary for an appropriate comment.

"Par exemple," he said.

Eventually, a wrench was found, and the fishing resumed. The pond narrowed to become a creek, with fins flickering on the edges and in pools in the mud. Some fish were caught by small, muddy boys skulking in the woods and darting out for illegal forays. In a rusty drum over a wood fire, carp and tench were cooking in red wine seasoned by bacon and onions—a meurette, or Burgundian fish stew. At noontime, a squad of men slogged down the creek dragging sticks, chasing the stragglers into the sluice. Then it was closed, and all hands lined up to take their pay in fish, eat the meurette, and drink a keg of Burgundy.

A ton of fish was sold by the pond owner to a dealer, who hauled it off to market. He said the carp would go to London, for sale to Chinese and Indian restaurants. The smaller fish went back into the pond again, with a rendezvous for two years from now. There was one final rite, centuries old. Mr. Untel picked up the day's biggest catch, a fat, golden carp weighing some 15 pounds, patted its heaving sides, and tossed it back into the pond.

"We always do that," he said, "for luck, next time."

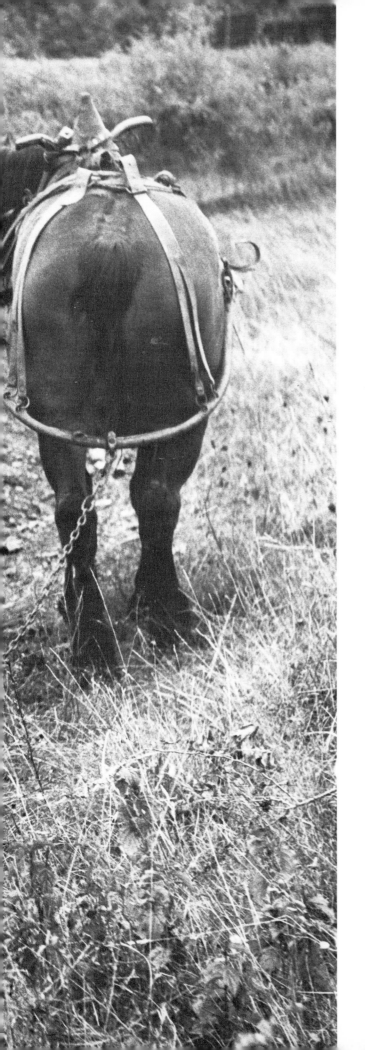

MAKING WAY FOR THE BRIOCHE

Paris—June, 1966

When the village of Merinchal in central France celebrated its saint's day this June, Mayor Pierre Ventenant, the baker, decided to do something special. He kneaded up a brioche nine feet wide and weighing 143 pounds, slid it into the oven, and reserved a place on the square for it to be sold for the benefit of the World Campaign Against Hunger.

But the cake rose higher than the oven door. The Mayor summoned the village masons and ordered them to demolish the front of his oven. The brioche went on sale as scheduled.

If the villagers have no bread tomorrow morning, they can follow the advice of Marie Antoinette, who was quoted, precisely, as having said, "Let them eat brioche."

Part Four   **LA TABLE**

A MENU TO DRIVE BY

Paris—1969

The Association of Master Cooks of France has appealed to the authorities to combat a seditious campaign holding that "gastronomy and automobile driving are basically incompatible." The idea that a meal fit for a Frenchman makes him unfit for the road was promulgated by Sécurité Routière, a safety organization. In a recent advertisement, it published the photograph of a man at a well-laid table with the caption: "In an hour, this gentleman will be driving at 140 an hour."

This was kilometers, of course, which puts the putative speed of the diner at 87 miles an hour. It says a great deal about French attitudes toward driving that in the debate that ensued, neither side raised the question whether the gentleman should be driving at 87 miles an hour, in a country with few speedways and one of the worst highway death rates in the world. The safety promoters and the chefs alike tacitly presumed that normal driving is an athletic exploit that calls for the reflexes of a toreador.

Sécurité Routière's ad began on a note of reproach:

"How often are you told: 'You must stop there, they have a marvelous gras-double [tripe] à la lyonnaise . . .' or yet: 'For 12 francs [$2], you get hors d'oeuvre, entrée, main dish, cheese, dessert, and a little beaujolais to write home about.'

"All that is tempting.

"Admit that you let yourself be tempted.

"Then, with lids drooping, eyes dull, the mind dozing, the reflexes slowed, you leave, just like that, at the wheel, taken by a lovely euphoria. Whatever the speed, it's always too fast when

you're in that shape. It's at that moment that you can kill somebody or be killed.

"Stupidly.

"France is a wonderful country for gastronomy, but gastronomy and automobile driving are basically incompatible.

"Good.

"So, take a light meal, otherwise you risk finishing your digestion in the hospital."

Leaders of the Master Cooks, a league of French chef-restauranteurs, angrily discussed the ad at a meeting in Paris. They instructed their president, Lucien Ogier, to take countermeasures.

At his handsome roadside inn, L'Aubergade in Pontchartrain, chef Ogier nowadays serves mainly what he describes as a fairly austere meal of four courses, which might be crayfish tails in a cheese sauce, chicken with morels in cream, a bit of cheese, and his own ice cream dessert. A small white wine or champagne might do for the whole meal, though some diners might switch to a red at the chicken or cheese.

"A man might feel a little heavy at table, but not when he's ready to leave," the chef said. "It wouldn't be the wine, anyway—it's the whiskey. Besides, people are in too much of a hurry to eat well nowadays. The five- or six-course meal is gone, except now and then in the hunting season."

"Anyway," he added, "we are only 20 minutes from the Arc de Triomphe. [Pontchartrain is 25 miles from Paris.] A client of mine, driving home, is just as safe as if he had dined in the Bois de Boulogne."

In his countercampaign, chef Ogier obtained statistics from the Paris prefecture of police on

82

the hourly frequency of accidents, and on the hourly incidence of alcohol in the blood of drivers. These charts appeared to show that the alcohol level reached its peak before dining, not afterward.

Armed with these charts, chef Ogier addressed urgent appeals to the tourist ministry, the prefecture, and the trade press for a counterdrive against a "systematic propaganda tending to damage our profession by inciting Frenchmen to avoid meals in order to stay alive."

So far, Sécurité Routière has guarded a prudent silence.

The chef's thesis was supported by a court case in southwest France. A motorist, arrested for weaving all over the road, told the court he had become dizzy not because he had drunk too much, but because he had eaten too little.

He was released with the warning: Don't drive if you've had one dish too few.

THE QUICK AND THE FED

Paris—April, 1967

Frenchmen have long held it to be self-evident that speed and gastronomy do not mix. Faced with a choice, more and more of them are opting for speed.

Not long ago, a quick lunch took something like two hours. Now, two hours is what it's supposed to take to drive from Paris to Avallon, 140 miles on the new autoroute. Formerly, this was a day's run, partly at the wheel but mostly at the table, preferably at the Hôtel de la Poste in Avallon, where a good night's rest was obligatory after a proper dinner of four to six courses, accompanied by a proper amount of fine wine.

Its octogenarian wine steward liked to say that he once saw a man commit suicide by drinking a glass of milk. Recently, he has been seen serving Coca-Cola from a silver ice bucket.

The Poste had three stars in the *Guide Michelin*—meaning that it was worth a special trip just to eat there—until last month, when it was demoted to two stars—worth only a detour. When the autoroute is extended past Avallon, it is apparent that many travelers will no longer trouble to make the detour. The contract for building speedway feeding stations—France has none, so far—has been assigned to a Parisian banking syndicate, which said in its opening announcement, "One does not take the autoroute to practice gastronomy." The emphasis will be on speed and price, with "snack bar" meals starting at a dollar.

The modern notion that time is money has long since infiltrated the area where gastronomy begins, in food production. A fine Bordeaux used to spend at least three years in the barrel and perhaps 10 more in the bottle before it was considered ready to drink. Now, two years in the barrel is pretty much a maximum, and a good château wine may be found on menus soon after it has been bottled.

In the Marne Valley, a new plant turns out cheese in a fast, continuous strip like a steel mill. In Brittany, where countrywomen still wear lace bonnets and wooden shoes, an inventor has built a machine to make crêpes. From this it is only a step to making food from petroleum, and an oil company here is doing precisely that. The product is being fed to cattle now, but the company is aiming higher.

The synthesizers still have a long way to go, however, to suppress the French love for a good table and the time to enjoy it. A popular bistro here thrives on the true story of the prominent client who arrived early but without a reservation, and begged the owner to give him a place, promising to eat quickly and move on. The owner told him, "Nobody eats quickly in my house," and threw him out.

GUIDE MICHELIN

Paris—March, 1970

The Hotel George V, which recently switched from French to Scottish beef, has been demoted from two Michelin stars to one. The Riviera, after a decade of gastronomic retrogression, can once again boast a three-star restaurant. It is also the first three-star in history where it may be difficult to end a repast with a bit of cheese—a phenomenon fraught with significance.

The foregoing are among the revelations of the new *Guide Michelin*, whose annual appearance in March is awaited with trepidation by French restaurateurs and with eager anticipation by gourmands everywhere.

The George V was acquired in 1968 by Charles Forte, the British cafeteria tycoon, but its demotion does not seem to have been inspired by chauvinism. The nearby Plaza-Athenée, which Mr. Forte bought at the same time, has preserved its two stars. Furthermore, two utterly French restaurants of the Belle Epoque, the elegant Laurent in the Champs-Elysées and the richly Toulouse-Lautrec-ish Escargot Montorgueil near

Les Halles, were also demoted from two stars to one.

Jean Berca, manager of the George V, said the downgrading caught him by surprise. "Just lately," Mr. Berca said, "we have taken to importing the best food products"—a statement that might raise any French eyebrow. He cited his switch from Charolais beef to Aberdeen Angus. There are of course many grades of Charolais, but the change may have marked a step up in quality and snob appeal. It ignored, however, the most highly regarded French beef, the Limousin. The demotion of the George V came with less surprise to resident foodlovers than to Mr. Berca. It was

suggested to him that some Michelin official might have been obliged to attend one of the large banquets that are a major function of the hotel. Mr. Berca replied that that would hardly be fair.

In awarding a third star to L'Oasis at La Napoule, near Cannes, Michelin paid a rare tribute to the late Fernand Point, the renowned chef of La Pyramide at Vienne. There are only 12 three-star restaurants and chef Jean-Pierre Outhier of L'Oasis is the third cook trained by Point to reach this pinnacle in recent years.

During a recent visit to L'Oasis, the Point influence was apparent from the first dish, a mousse à la rascasse, which was a Pyramide

86

recipe elegantly adapted to the unlikely Mediterranean hogfish. This ingredient was the only concession to the Provençale in a classic menu that ended with the opulent lyonnais array of desserts on serving carts. However, when the diner asked for a bit of cheese to accompany the last of an excellent little Bandol wine, he was told that there was none. The waiter explained that the region did not produce a worthwhile cheese, that it was impossible to keep cheese in the heat of Provence, and that the customers did not want it. Dining experiences elsewhere on the Côte d'Azur demonstrated that only the last explanation had some validity.

Meals at L'Oasis are copious and—another Point influence—inexpensive for what they offer, ranging from $6 to $9. The most expensive menu today, for example, consisted of new asparagus (hot or cold, with choice of four sauces), fresh salmon in cream, canard a l'orange, and all the dessert one could cope with. In the good old days, a menu like that or even considerably longer would not be complete without cheese before dessert or as dessert. The old French dictum is that a meal without cheese is like a day without sunshine. In a parochial school in the Southwest, an old priest still recites to his pupils a rhyme of his own composition: "Cheese, ah, poetry, perfume of our meal; if we didn't have it, how would life feel?" This is still the view of the old, the rustic, and the humble. But in the smart feeding places of Paris and the Côte d'Azur, cheese is more and more neglected, except when it turns up in a fondue or a pizza.

Invited to comment on his elevation, Mr. Outhier said: "It's very satisfying of course. But it's upsetting, too, because it's very hard to live up to. There is nothing more to win, or to hope for."

THE SELF-ROASTING COOKBOOK

Paris—April, 1969

A book that pans itself has been published, inadvertently it would seem, by Time-Life, Inc.

The product, as they call it in Rockefeller Center, is the French edition of *The Cooking of Provincial France*. This was the first of a series of cookbooks being prepared by the Time-Life organization for marketing by subscription. No expense was spared. When the American edition appeared a year ago, Craig Claiborne, the food critic of *The New York Times*, reported the jest, "They're throwing money around like it was rice."

Time-Life Books hired some of the best-known talent in the United States, under the supervision of Mrs. M.F.K. Fisher, Michael Field, and Julia Child, and teams of photographers under Mark Kauffman. A huge affair was thrown

87

in New York to greet the product. The same day, Mr. Claiborne warned that when the French edition was published, Franco-American relations were "very likely to get worse. They might even start a small war." "I might very well join them," Mr. Claiborne added.

Following this warning, Time-Life engaged at a substantial fee—the only kind of fee involved in the project—France's most feared gastronomic critic, Robert J. Courtine, one of whose pen names is le Grincheux—the surly one. Mr. Courtine was asked to write an introduction and some notes to the French edition. Nobody in Time-Life who was reachable here acknowledges having read the copy.

Time-Life rented one of the pavilions at Les Halles to introduce the edition last month. It erected a striped and carpeted circus tent, ordered food from half a dozen countries (some of it authentic and some good), brought over from New York many of those responsible for the book, hired some models in see-through dresses, and invited the Tout-Paris. Each departing guest got a sample of the product. It was only weeks later that people here began reading the footnotes. Actually, the indignant authors in New York seem to have raised the alarm first. When word got around, *La Cuisine des Provinces de France* became an item for collectors of curiosa.

The notes are a running, heckling commentary on the book. Here is Mr. Courtine's comment on the recipe for crêpes gratinées, stuffed with mushrooms and diced chicken, or ham and artichoke, or shrimp, et al.

"That's a lot of work for a skimpy result! It's the typical dish supposed to surprise and charm a foreign woman, but it is fake grand cuisine and as antigastronomic as can be."

The corrections, scoldings, and amendments begin at the first page, and make up something of a cookbook themselves. Rebuking the authors, Mr. Courtine advises that the cotriade, a fish soup, "is in fact not at all spiced"; that a dish *à la champagne* certainly does use bubbly wine, for that's what it's about; that you can no longer, alas, get mountain trout and crayfish in every alpine auberge (they've been long since outlawed). Where the authors say a quiche lorraine should be followed by a cold bird, Mr. Courtine remarks, "Why the devil should it?" On the instruction "make an omelette for each guest," he comments patiently, "You can very well make a successful omelette for 3 or 4," and he explains how.

Mr. Courtine advises that hors d'oeuvres are "more varied than the author thinks" and usually not spicy, that rather than "judge the quality of a restaurant on the terrine maison," the real gourmet "will shun it like a plague." In fact, he adds gently, the coarse popular terrines despised by the author are likely to be better than the fancy ones. Where the book advises that one should not roast game birds, Mr. Courtine adds simply: "Except partridge, pheasant, quail, etc." The "etc." helps explain his pen name, le Grincheux.

Other helpful but contradictory hints: "Classic mayonnaise does not contain mustard. . . . There is no cream in 'true' hollandaise. . . . You must not put garlic in onion soup. . . . If the peas are fresh, there is no need to blanch them. . . . Nobody would dream of adding croutons to tripes. . . . One rarely lards a Charolais roast. . . ."

Mr. Courtine tries to be kind and broadminded, in his fashion. "Before smiling at the several failings of this book," he advises the French reader, think what a cookbook on America might be, written by a scrupulous and foodloving Frenchman." He even contradicts the authors' praise of French rice, and commends American processed rice instead. Blows are softened by the phrase "the author seems to have confused . . ." or "the author has perhaps confused . . ." But Mr. Courtine is harsh about the book's failings on wine. "To recommend a big wine with Roquefort is a grave error," he declares.

When, near the end, an author recounts an evidently favorite story about slipping three cloves of garlic into a salad without the guest's knowledge, the critic galumphs: "It seems doubtful to me that the garlic taste would quite disappear."

Rumors circulating in Paris and London talk of heads rolling because of what is called Time-Life's publishing gaffe. The local office of Time-Life Books, disclaiming responsibility, referred queries to New York headquarters.

Mr. Courtine in a telephone interview confirmed that he had received reproaches from Time-Life since the book appeared, but said he couldn't imagine why. He had done the job he was paid for, he said.

"I think it's rather amusing," he said. "I hope they'll see it that way, too."

LE SCANDALE DE LA SAUCE BEARNAISE

Paris—January, 1971

One of the problems the European Common Market seems unable to solve is how to make a Sauce Béarnaise. Any good cook can make one, and any *bonne fourchette* or, as it turns out, any *feinschmecker* can identify the golden sauce melting on, say, a rare fillet of Charolais. But after more than a year of *dégustation*, the functionaries in Brussels and the six governments they serve have been unable to agree on the recipe.

To the chagrin of French gastronomy, the dossier was opened by the Academy of Cuisine of West Germany. It complained that certain canners, notably in France, were marketing "sauce béarnaise" using olive oil, lard, or even peanut oil instead of butter.

Scandal.

Learning of this *démarche*, the Académie Culinaire de France joined its German brethren in asking that the Common Market, in its effort to harmonize the laws of member nations on food products, decree that a sauce without butter was not béarnaise. The French academicians were further embarrassed to learn that their own Government had been taking the side of olive oil et al. They lowered their gunsights from Brussels to Paris, with a broadside demanding to know "why unscrupulous French businessmen are undermining the professional patrimony of French cooks."

After a climactic conference with a delegation of chefs, the Agriculture Ministry modified its position before the Common Market. Pointing out that (a) some gastronomic authorities acknowledged the existence of a béarnaise made with olive oil and (b) some French canners had been marketing such a product for "quite a long

89

time," the ministry now considered that (a) béarnaise should be made of butter, but (b) a béarnaise with olive oil should be allowed "transitionally" provided that the label said "béarnaise à l'huile."

Jean Germa, the 72-year-old chef who is secretary general of the Académie Culinaire, predicted that "béarnaise with oil" would be banned when existing stocks were used up. A minor victory, he allowed. "I don't see very well how a sauce in a jar can keep its freshness," he said with a shrug. Mr. Germa acknowledged that some authors had fallen into error on the béarnaise, because olive oil is the staple of the southwestern province of Béarn. Mr. Germa stands on the "classic" recipe as given among others by Escoffier—who describes the Béarnaise as "basically a mayonnaise made with butter."

Mayonnaise is, of course, a sauce made of egg yolk, olive oil, and vinegar or lemon juice—although in the United States, which is not a member of the Common Market, these ingredients may not correspond with the contents of the jar. The béarnaise is made with a reduction of wine vinegar (or wine, or wine and vinegar) and shallots, to which yolk and then butter are added, all flavored with chervil and tarragon. It is served lukewarm ("Don't dream of serving this sauce hot," says Escoffier) on steak and other hot dishes. He assigned the honor of inventing the béarnaise to Maître Collinet, who either was a brilliantly inventive chef or had a brilliantly inventive press agent. Collinet kept an inn called the Henri IV at St. Germain-en-Laye west of Paris. He is widely credited with having invented not only the sauce béarnaise but also that extraordinary feat of deep fat frying, the pomme soufflé. In the Collinet legend, the béarnaise is presumed to have gotten its name from that of Collinet's restaurant—Henri IV having been a son of Béarn. The spud story is more circumstantial.

When the first train was chugging from Paris to St. Germain in 1837 (so 'tis said), Maître Collinet put his sliced potatoes to fry for the notables who were coming. But the pioneer locomotive had trouble climbing the grade, and the guests were late. Collinet sadly pulled his potatoes out and then, when the train finally arrived, returned them, half-cooked, to the hot fat. Eureka. They puffed into golden shells of hot air. Collinet and his potatoes are a legend worthy of Newton and his apple. Unromantic researchers, however, have found recipes for sauce béarnaise and pomme soufflé in publications that unfortunately antedate Collinet and his restaurant.

The ability of legend to survive hard fact is especially tenacious in the world of gastronomy where, generally, cooks cannot write and writers cannot cook. An example is the sauce Armoricaine, or Américaine. But that is another story.

CRISIS IN HORSEMEAT

Paris—October, 1967

The Minister of Information ate horsemeat on television, but Joseph Faviot, the horse butcher in the Marché St. Honoré, was not sure it would do much good. Sitting in front of his deserted shop, under the three gilded horseheads, Mr. Faviot watched customers passing him by and said, "It's catastrophic." The crisis, the worst in the trade since horsemeat was legalized in 1830, began with two outbreaks of food poisoning attributed to chopped horsemeat. The publicity caused a slump in horsemeat consumption now estimated at as much as 80 percent.

Since the first commercial slaughterhouse for horses was opened here 100 years ago, horsemeat had grown steadily in public acceptance. At first, this was largely because it was cheap. Then belief spread that horsemeat was fortifying to the blood, and prices climbed.

Mr. Faviot's best chopped horsemeat was offered today at $1.20 a pound, while in a neighboring shop the best chopped beef was selling at 90 cents. Despite the price, horsemeat continues to bear the stigma of poverty, and it is almost never seen on the menus of restaurants. In homes it may be eaten in steaks, roasts, and sausage (mixed with pork or beef), but often it is just chopped, and served raw with onions and other seasoning, the dish being known as steak tartare.

This was a factor in the food poisoning cases here. Hygienic rules in France are in some ways more stringent than in the United States—for example, chopped meat must be ground before the customer. However, a butcher who sold the tainted meat in question confessed that he had mixed old scraps with fresh ones. He was jailed.

Following emergency meetings of horse butchers and local politicians, a luncheon was held at Vaugirard this afternoon with Minister of Information Georges Gorse as the guest of honor and horse as the *pièce de résistance*. The minister is described by an associate as a connoisseur of beef—a man who knows his cuts to the point that he can shame his supplier into selling him a "pelican," a rare bit of fillet normally saved by butchers for their own tables. Mr. Gorse rose to the occasion. He ate horse tripe sausage, horse roast, and raw chopped horsemeat, with the help of a muscadet and a volnay—a white Loire wine and a red burgundy, respectively. Afterward, he said it was all delicious and he felt fine.

In his shop, Mr. Flaviot remained gloomy. "I don't think horsemeat will ever come back, because it's too dear," he said. He was bitter about the press. "When an airplane crashes, they don't talk about it for ten days, do they?" he demanded.

A blonde woman entered and ordered 500 grams (1.1 pounds) of chopped meat. She glared at a visiting reporter and said, "Shameful! Making the butchers pay for other people's mistakes. Me, I think it's all politics." She stalked out without another word.

Another woman came by, leading a dachshund on a leash. "Is there any news?" she asked Mr. Flaviot. She said she had bought horsemeat from him twice a week for seven years, for her dog. "But I'm afraid to give it to her now."

Mr. Flaviot waited impassively until she had left. Then he said, "If this goes on, I'll close up shop and take up a pick and shovel."

TWILIGHT OF THE GOLDEN LOAF

Paris—May, 1966

The end may be approaching for one of the most endearing aspects of the daily scene in France—the long, bare, golden loaf of bread tucked under the arm or peering from the net bag of the housewife, the businessman, the schoolgirl, and the boy on the bike.

The French baking industry—or craft, rather—has been shaken by a new venture of Générale Alimentaire. In a country whose food, the most delicious in the western world, is still mainly produced by independent artisans, this corporation has been growing by mergers to the point where last year it sold $56 million worth of packaged foods. Now it is building what may best be described as a bread mill in Besançon in eastern France. Strips of dough will flow like steel ingots on a belt through a "tunnel oven." The emerging bread will be chilled, packaged, and sold from Alsace to Burgundy.

Industrial baking is not unknown in France, but heretofore it has been limited to rectangular loaves of the American type, and packaged toast, cakes, and cookies, none of which have been very successful. What is new about the Besançon project is that it proposes to package standard French loaves such as the *baguette*, a 10-ounce, two-foot wand; the *bâtard*, which is half as long and twice as wide; and the *deux-livres*, which is just as long and twice as wide. Also on the program are rolls, croissants, and brioches, those staples of the French breakfast—all to be wrapped for the first time. Even more revolutionary is the fact that G.A. has persuaded many bakers in the region—30 percent, according to trade sources—to let their ovens go cold forever when the plant opens this fall, and become sales outlets for factory breads. If the project is successful, Générale Alimentaire plans to repeat it in other regions. Does this mean the end of the baker-artisan? What will happen to the quality of French bread? Inquiries at the baking industry pavilion of the annual Paris fair, handily adjoining the sausage and wine stands, brought out wide agreement that French bread was not what it used to be.

Three major reasons were cited: The quality of flour has declined as land productivity has been raised by new seed varieties and synthetic fertilizer; bakers are growing more careless and their equipment is aging, and finally the use of old-fashioned leaven has disappeared except in the most backward regions of France.

In the old days, the baker would set aside a piece of dough, sometimes called the "mother," from each mixing and add it to the next. This leavening is slow, but according to connoisseurs it adds a wonderful flavor. Now, bakers use brewers' yeast and often add ascorbic acid to speed the rising.

A manufacturer of small bakery ovens warned smilingly that he was biased because the Besançon project was a menace to his business. Then he commented, "In theory, a big bakery can make good bread. In practice, no. Baking is an art, depending on hundreds of details. A good baker buys good flour and works hard. Men paid by the hour just don't care. I live in a new suburb where the planners have allowed only one bakery, which is thus big enough to afford a tunnel oven. The bread is disastrous."

Additives to keep bread fresh are forbidden by French law, but a big company will have to do something to avoid having a fatal proportion of unsold bread. The small baker knows his clients' demand within a dozen loaves.

In a Paris shop this morning, a tired and dusty baker was handing baguettes to a queue of customers. They would point to the stock of loaves, ranging from a dark brown to pale gold and choose one. He would squeeze it (crackle) as he handed it to the customer who would squeeze too (crackle). He had heard about the Besançon project, the baker said. He couldn't care less.

"We are through anyhow," he said with a shrug. "With wheat going up every year and the baguette still frozen at 44 centimes."

French bakers take some comfort and even amusement in the fact that midget baguettes are flown from Paris to New York and sold, in plastic wrappers, for something like 4 francs.

93

[For all my cries of alarm, those years in France were a movable feast indeed. I suppose the greatest meal of all, in every sense, was a six-hour orgy at the Troisgros in Roanne, which many think is the finest restaurant in the world. It was still relatively unknown in early 1966 when a group of food writers led by Jean Didier of the Guide Kleber descended from Paris to confer an award. Briefly, the presentation luncheon was preceded by an apéritif of Sancerre, accompanied by hot tripe sausage, foie gras, and Alpine crayfish. At table, we began with raw truffles thinly sliced with artichoke heart in vinaigrette, followed by one of the Troisgros brothers' most brilliant achievements: thin fillets of Loire salmon in a light sorrel sauce.

An unsweetened sherbet in champagne prepared the diner for a dandelion and bacon salad, then a rib roast of Charolais beef in a Beaujolais sauce that had been simmering for days. Petits fours and a hot apple tart finished the luncheon. The wines were Puligny-Montrachet, Château Petrus, and the house Gevrey-Chambertin, served in pewter pitchers.

Mr. Didier, "unaccountably slender and fresh," as I wrote at the time, smilingly drove off with his colleagues to dine at Bocuse in Lyons. My wife and I tottered off to bed, determined to fast for a week. Next day, we paused to say hello to a peasant friend in Morgon, in the Beaujolais. Nothing would do but that we had to take *fortune du pot*, with the peasant's wife in an agony of anxiety lest we fail to clear our plates. Pot luck included, as we shall never forget, Lyonnais sausage in brioche, rabbit, chicken, and duck.

Just to prove that this was no regional aberration, here is part of a dispatch from the Anjou.]

A VINTNER'S LUNCH

Beaulieu-sur-Layon—June, 1964

If French gourmandise is on the decline, it was not evident at a vintner's wedding luncheon here the other day.

The menu: Langoustines, boned stuffed chicken in aspic, poached salmon of the Loire with beurre blanc, braised leg of veal, celery hearts, roast duck, spring salad, marquise (a cake) au Grand Marnier, and strawberries Melba.

The wines: As an apéritif, a 1914 Maison Faye, followed by champagne, a 1964 Cabernet rosé, a 1933 white Beaulieu, a 1934 white Beaulieu, a 1964 red Cabernet, a 1947 Clos du Paradis, and, finally, champagne and liqueurs.

All of the wines were, of course, Angevin except the champagne, for which Auguste Gouin, father of the groom, apologized as a modern convention at weddings. The old white wines were a brilliant gold, of an extraordinary mellow sweetness.

Mr. Gouin, whose own complexion is a tawny rosé, said the age of the wines was not exceptional; he recalled tasting an 1870 in his mother's caves, and there was still some 1881 left.

Mr. Gouin pointed out that, although he began his menu with a 1914, the climax of the luncheon was a 1947. That, he said, was really what one might call a "year of the century."

WINE: SUPPLE, FRUITY, EVEN SEDUCTIVE

Chateauneuf-du-Pape—February, 1965

Just a year ago, Minister of Agriculture Edgard Pisani, a winegrower himself, proclaimed 1964 as a vintage of the century. He considered, apparently, that the saying "in vino veritas"—in wine there is truth—refers to wine after it has been drunk, not before. Mr. Pisani's enthusiasm was widely publicized in the United States, and 1964 French wines have enjoyed enormous demand there, in spite of President Johnson's effort in behalf of the California product. But vintners from Bordeaux to Burgundy reply to questions about the crop with tolerant amusement.

A typical estimate was that of Pierre Raynaud, a stocky, grayhaired grower who is also deputy mayor of Chateauneuf-du-Pape, the best-known name in the Côtes du Rhone. Over a bottle of his own remarkable 1957, Mr. Raynaud said he would class 1964 as better than 1963 (a disaster year) and 1962, an average one, but not as good as 1961. In short, a "correct" wine, he said. In August last year, Mr. Raynaud conceded, the crop looked good. Then it rained during the harvest, with damaging effect. One of the most famous châteaus in Bordeaux, in fact, will bottle no 1964 wine under its own label. As always, a few individual fields produced really outstanding wines, but results everywhere were variable except in Champagne, where growers say 1964 really was a great vintage.

Mr. Raynaud explained that large crops seldom yielded the finest wines. "Thirty years ago," he said, "we made less than half as much wine per hectare as we do today, but it was better wine. We culled the grapes then—we used to pluck the bad ones from each bunch. If we did that now, we wouldn't have what to eat. We are crushed by taxes. We've got to raise production."

Villië-Morgon—November, 1968

It may be said on the very best authority that the premier growths of the 1964 Beaujolais wines are supple, fruity, and even seductive, well-balanced, musical, dégagé, amusing, warm, generous, and alive. They are agreeable yet profound, strong but not too serious—gay in fact—and they don't accuse their alcohol, which is high. They are neither oaken, horsy, or chewy. It may also be said, on the next-to-the-best authority, which is the growers themselves, that 1964 is far superior to 1963, surely as good as 1962, and possibly equal to 1959, if not better. It is not fair, however, to compare it to 1949, one grower said reproachfully, for "that was a holy wine."

97

The best authority is, of course, the wine itself. It was thoroughly sniffed, tasted, and drunk recently on the annual pilgrimage led by André Allard, the Left Bank restaurateur. For Mr. Allard, it was a serious affair, for some 10,000 of the 15,000 bottles of wine consumed every year in his small but famous establishment are Beaujolais. The rest are Burgundies; Mr. Allard, a Burgundian, holds that Bordeaux are all right, if taken on doctor's orders.

Despite the heady talk at harvest time of a "year of the century," Mr. Allard approached the test with peasant caution. The great years, he pointed out, have never been years of large crops. He warned, too, that the quality of the Beaujolais, which is the first of the important wines to become drinkable and the first to perish, did not necessarily have any bearing on the quality of other wines.

The day's work began in the kitchen of Pierre Augris at Villié-Morgon, with a fortifying breakfast of hot sausage, cheese, and a white Maconnais, to clear the palate. Mr. Augris, a middle-aged veteran of the Resistance whose father was a wine commissionaire before him, had sketched out an itinerary to cover what he considered the best caves in seven districts, starting from the lightest wines to the fruitiest. Thus, the party worked from Chiroubles to Fleurie to Moulin-a-Vent to St. Amour to Julienas to Morgon to Côte de Brouilly. The procedure in each was the same. The vintner would siphon wine from a barrel and pour it into the shallow silver tasting cups. Each visitor and the grower, too, would swirl the wine to admire its color, sniff it, then roll it on his tongue. The vintner would then proceed to another pressing from a different field.

Mr. Allard had warned against swallowing, for, he said, it took a clear head at the end of the day to remember and compare 25 wines or more. He was not seen to follow his advice. He and Mr. Augris, both lifelong tasters, began the day with

something of the ruby Beaujolais complexions typical of the region. Their companions did not achieve the same tint until nightfall. The talk became heady with fragrant adjectives and village verbs which, like some wines, do not travel. A visitor learned that, when the wine, or anything else, is working well in Morgon, it "morgons," or even "muguets," a verb coined from the beloved lily of the valley. In Julienas it may "prunet," from the prune. A wine could be too "carpentered," whatever that may be, or too "horsy," because, like horsemeat, it grows soft with age.

The aging of Beaujolais, it developed, is a tender subject. Georges Abel, mayor of Chenasse, demonstrated in his vast cave at Moulin-a-Vent a very good bottle of 10-year-old Beaujolais, which he called virtually a Burgundy. Mr. Allard smiled a Burgundian smile and said, "You Beaujolais are all chauvinists. You are always saying your best wines are almost Burgundies. It's a nice wine, but a Beaujolais should be a Beaujolais and a Burgundy a Burgundy."

At the end of each visit, Mr. Augris lingered to fill a bottle or two from a barrel, chosen apparently by unspoken agreement with Mr. Allard. The bottles came out at lunch, following a guinea hen in a village restaurant in Julienas, and again at dinner, which featured hen with morels at the Chapon Fin in Thoissey. The wines again were compared, with Mr. Augris endeavoring to keep their origin secret. Except for this journalist, nobody was fooled. In the end, Mr. Allard chose to repeat last year's purchase of a Côte de Brouilly for use beginning next spring, and he decided to order a St. Amour to serve as a new wine, beginning with the New Year.

The purchase of the St. Amour required a return visit, long after dark, to the cave of François Spay. The stocky, elderly farmer greeted the party in his yard with a shout of joy. Mr. Spay demonstrated his nickname, Two-Legged Barrel, by thrusting open the door of his cave with his midriff, and hastened to his best pressing. There, with his siphon working steadily, he engaged in a long, loud, half-serious haggle over prices with Mr. Allard, and a chaffing match with his other guests, touching on his fecundity—Mr. Spay is the father of 12—the Leftist politics of Mr. Augris, and the virtues of France and sins of the French.

Mr. Allard did not concede on the price until the third or fourth round of tasting. This called for several more. The farmer boasted to a parting visitor, "You know, the old pastor himself always said, 'That Spay loves his wine.'"

THE COGNAC WAR

Cognac—February, 1972

The thirst of Americans, Britons, and overseas Chinese for the finer things of life has provoked a conflict known around here as "La Petite Guerre du Cognac." "War" is perhaps a strong word for a commotion in which nobody is feeling any pain except, possibly, that innocent bystander the consumer. This is ironic because each side insists that its dearest aim is to protect the public interest. The battlefield is the gentle valley of the Charente, a broad region north of Bordeaux that produces an unpalatable white wine which, by a miracle of distillation, is transformed into the noblest brandy of them all.

In the heart of the region, around the town of Cognac, are the prime districts known as La Grande Champagne and La Petite Champagne,

not to be confused with the home of the bubbly far to the east. A 50–50 blend of the two is called cognac fine champagne, or fine (feen) for short. Nobody seriously questions its superiority, but that is what the fight is all about. In one corner are the great merchant houses—Martell, Hennessy, and Courvoisier—backed to a degree by the grower associations of the four less-favored districts. In the other are the merchant house of Rémy-Martin and the growers of grande and petite champagne. The problem is that they've all been doing too well. Sales of cognac have quadrupled since the war, while production has gone up about two-and-a-half times. The result was inevitable: Shippers could hold down the demand by raising prices, or satisfy it by adding more of the lesser cognacs to

99

their blends, and by selling them younger. In some cases, they are alleged to have done both. "The question now is whether to plant still more vines, in order to hold prices down, or to control the demand by letting prices rise," said a taster for the merchant firm of Denis-Mounié. In any event, prices have indeed soared, although output has been pushed faster than some purists would like.

"The quality of all the big labels has declined," said Jean Danflou, a Paris dealer in fine brandies. Denis Lahana, the chef of Chez Denis, added, "A three-star cognac today is not equal to the two-star they sold before the war."

Two-star cognac is no more. Three-star is the minimum now and accounts for 90 percent of sales. Legally, it represents cognac that has been aged in the wood at least 18 months; in practice, it may be aged rather longer, and usually some old cognac is added to perfume the blend. ("Napoleon Brandy" is, incidentally, a promotional fantasy. The product so advertised was never purveyed to the Bonapartes and has no legal definition as to contents.)

The war broke into the open in the fall of 1970, when the big three dropped the words fine champagne from their labels. They still insist that most of the cognac in their blends comes from the top growths. But, while 1970 produced the biggest crop in a century, they argue that the supply must be eked out with selected brandies from the lesser districts to meet the demand. Spokesmen for the growers of grande and petite champagne called a news conference at which they charged "certain firms" with lowering the quality of the merchandise. Rémy-Martin, the spiritual leader, so to speak, of the movement, began advertising the superiority of fine champagne. Envoys of all factions met here last spring and signed a peace pact, pledging to shun all publicity casting any reflection on any kind of cognac. But nothing basic had been decided and in the fall, hostilities

flared again. The growers of "fine" stormed out of the Cognac Producers' Federation, charging that the top districts were getting shortchanged in the allocation of permits to increase plantings.

This is part of the conflict between quality and quantity. The big houses feel that the surface planted in vines should be increased hugely over coming years. The growers worry that they may be caught with a glut some day—but meanwhile, they want their fair shares of the valuable planting rights. Robert Charpentier, Mayor of Brie-sous-Archiac and owner of one of the finest vineyards in Cognac, acknowledged, "The attachment we used to have to quality is being abandoned." Pierre Seguinot, another prosperous grower at La Nerolle, said that the increased use of fertilizer and insecticides, which has more than doubled average output per acre since the war, has damaged the product—and the soil.

"We must follow progress," he said apologetically. "They use more fertilizer now to grow more grain; certainly the bread is not as good. The same with wine—and automobiles. I'm trying to farm more naturally, with as much humus as I can get. I find our soil becoming asphyxiated by the lack of bacterial life."

The houses of Mr. Charpentier and Mr. Seguinot are typical Cognac homesteads, stonewalled squares with no window facing out, a precaution attributed to the wars of religion. They contrast sharply with such Hennessy homes as the Château de St. Brice, where Catherine de Medici is said to have persuaded Henry IV that Paris was worth a mass, and where Killian Hennessy now resides with his wife, and his son and her daughter by previous marriages, who married each other last year. The first Hennessy to sell cognac was Richard, a soldier from County Cork in the service of Louis XV. "No, not a mercenary," said a Hennessy aide in gentle reproof. "I'd say rather a gentleman of fortune." After the Revolution, the Hennessy stock was

blended in succeeding generations by marriage with daughters of the impoverished nobility, so that today all its scions are titled.

The plebeian Irish name may help explain, however, Hennessy's dominant position in the American market. It is so entrenched there that during Prohibition, when rum runners used to rendezvous off the islands of St. Pierre et Miquelon, wags proposed to change their name to St. Pierre et Hennessy. Gerald de Geoffre, the present head of the firm and a Hennessy on his mother's side, remarked that contrary to popular belief, "in your country cognac is also the drink of ethnic minorities." This applies, too, to the Chinese of Hong Kong and Singapore, who collectively are the fourth largest market for cognac, after Britain, the United States, and West Germany.

The Hennessys argue that blending of selected plebeian cognacs with the nobler growths need not harm the product. Gilles Hennessy, the newest member of the firm, said, "Fine champagne meant something 30 years ago. Today, it doesn't mean a thing." He explained that output per hectare had risen two-and-one-half times, implying that quality had suffered.

Mr. Seguinot, the independent grower, scoffed at the contention of the big houses that they are maintaining quality by blending old brandies and choice newer stock. Warehouse and farm supplies now, he pointed out, equal only four years of consumption.

"The cognac war is really a commercial quarrel between merchants, speaking in the name of the peasants," said Georges Flusin, a manager of the Chambre d'Agriculture here. "There is a confusion abroad about labels. You can order a Martell in some countries, thinking you are getting a cognac, and what you get is a foreign brandy. If cognac becomes like any brandy, then we are lost."

Part Five **LE FOLKLORE**

WHEN A FRENCHMAN TAKES THE WHEEL

Generalizations should be avoided like traffic tickets, but Frenchmen who are professionally concerned with motorists agree, not without a certain pride, that the French driver is the most unruly in the world. An even harsher view was expressed by Roger Lapeyre, who gave up his own car six years ago when he founded the association called Rights of the Pedestrian. "The driver in Europe, and above all in France, is a killer," he said in an interview. "The car has become a means of power. Many who have no satisfaction in life find it behind the wheel. They shed the vicissitudes of life, they want to pass, to be the strongest, to insult others."

Another big problem, he went on, is laxity in enforcement of the laws. "It's hard for an American to understand," he said with a smile, "but in France a traffic policeman likes to verbalize. And if he writes a ticket, one out of three will pay a fine. Everybody has got a friend of a friend."

Mr. Lapeyre said his organization had won some fights, such as for traffic lights and signs to be made visible to pedestrians, and lost some, such as the elimination of a footpath along the Seine in favor of a speedway. The group is now international, he said, but an American affiliate went broke. The French group, Mr. Lapeyre recounted, lost a few prosperous members because the officers turned down their pet proposal, which was that they smash windows of cars parked at street crossings—or at least that they paint the windows black. "And yet," he added, "there are times when one can understand. . ."

At the American Automobile Association's bureau on Rue de la Paix, a French employee said the motor tourist's first impression of Paris was "awful" and "we have to explain that it's not the same all over Europe." But Rome's streets and traffic are even worse, she added. She said the typical tourist was well advised to park his car and see Paris by Metro. Discourtesy, she suggested, is not limited to French drivers. Inquiries often are made about American license numbers taken from cars leaving the scene of an accident. Down the street at the Royal Auto Club, in Place Vendôme, another Frenchwoman offered this defense: "It's said that Paris drivers are not as courteous as they should be, but can they afford to be? When I drive I feel as they do, and when I am afoot, I feel as the pedestrians do."

She conceded that English drivers were more disciplined. She gave part of the credit to the fact that nobody has the right of way in Britain, whereas "here, anybody coming from the right side thinks he can damage your car." Thus a farmer coming from a dirt road will charge onto a larger road with firm righteousness, she acknowledged. Contrary to popular beliefs, she added, rustics were worse than city drivers, because "they think the country belongs to them." "I think there are very few really good drivers," she concluded.

Upstairs at the French Auto Club, Georges Trubert opined that "lack of courtesy and

negligence has to do with the French character." This, he said, is "rather to be a critic of authority, to be reckless, to find a way to get out of the rules —they are for others, not me."

Jacques Remy, spokesman for the highway safety organization, Prevention Routière, had studied the question statistically and as a tourist,

and drawn some sharp conclusions. First, he said, French drivers are not the deadliest—Italians are. The latest available figures for killings per 100,000,000 kilometers traveled: Italy, 13.5; France, 9.2; West Germany, 8.4; United States, 3.2. He pulled out another table and demonstrated that Britain had far more accidents, but fewer deaths than France—though accidents and deaths were rising fast in both countries. He suggested that road conditions were one factor— autoroutes cut the accident rate by two-thirds, he declared—but national characteristics played a big part, too.

In America, Mr. Remy said, French visitors find the placidity and obedience to law almost amusing, and he thought he noted a dramatic difference when he crossed into Quebec. The French character, he explained.

"The German is not such a good driver," Mr. Remy said. "He drives fast, too. Of course, he has those autobahns.

"The Italian is a wonderful driver, a pilot, rather. He drives with brio—with dash. But when he has an accident, they pick him up in little pieces. In Rome, the driver measures the pedestrian's rate of speed and calculates his own to miss him. If the pedestrian changes, he's lost. In Paris, the driver doesn't watch for the pedestrian at all. Therefore, in Rome it is best to cross the street without looking and not to change your mind. In Paris, look out."

Mr. Remy said French law says drivers should yield to cars coming from the right, but that the public misinterprets this as meaning that if they are coming from the right side, they have an unlimited right of way. Similarly, he acknowledged, they think the turn indicator gives them the right to turn. "When the French think they have a right, nothing will stop them," he said.

On the other hand, he said, the Frenchman thinks "that sign is for boobs, not for an intelligent chap like me." For this reason, he said, the French highway authorities deliberately use very few stop signs, on the theory that familiarity would breed contempt. It all boils down, Mr. Remy said, to "System D," for the verb *debrouiller*—a reference to the French passion for working around things, including taxes and traffic rules.

"And yet," he told a parting guest, "it is not such a bad thing. During the Occupation, it kept us going. Studies have shown that in the German concentration camps, the French prisoners had the best survival record—morale, intelligence, escape, System D."

A CENTIME SAVED IS A CENTIME EARNED

Paris—October, 1964

If President de Gaulle wants to match the United States in every way that counts, he will simply have to do something about French thrift. To be sure, he is making a handsome effort with his *force de frappe*, but he can never hope to achieve the grandeur of American spending without a comparable contribution from the French citizenry.

He has a hard row to hoe. I pass over, as possibly extreme, the case of the Parisian who was arrested a while ago for pasting up the punch holes in Metro tickets. I salute, as only sensible, the sale of automobile collision insurance valid only on weekends, for weekend drivers. More illuminating, on the subject of parsimony, is the French light switch. I would suppose that no country has more switches per capita, or more ingenious ones. A favorite among bistro keepers is the one attached to the lock in the cabinet downstairs. The light goes on only when the lock has been turned, but you can't find the lock in the dark. Not amusing, but it saves electricity, *mon vieux*.

Even more common is the minuterie, or light switch timed to get one through the halls almost to the door. Actually, it is not possible to achieve the same result for all tenants, because the distance to be traveled varies. But the owner of a fairly expensive, five-story apartment house where I used to live solved this problem with a neat application of logic: the light was timed to go out as the ascenseur reached the third story. What electricity was wasted by the tenants on the lower floors was made up by those living above. (Speaking of ascenseurs, lifts or elevators, do those in other countries take their names so literally, and forbid passengers to ride them down?)

An appeal to French thrift is doubtless the motivation for the sign on many shop doors reading "Entrée Libre." The prices may be the highest in the Western world, but the admission is

107

free. One never, somehow, sees a sign reading "Sortie Libre." Seeking enlightenment, I asked an elderly Parisian lady of my acquaintance what Entrée Libre signified. She raised her eyebrows with that air of surprise that greets a foreigner here when he questions established folkways—for example, when he asks why the head of a numerous family should receive priority in boarding a bus. "Why," said the lady, "entrée libre means you are under no obligation to buy."

If that indeed is it, many salespeople have carried the policy one step further. They dare you just to try and buy something. But we digress. The subject was thrift, was it not?

Until recently, a Frenchman could save 5 centimes on a postcard if he kept the message down to five words. Then the Government repealed the privilege, ostensibly because it cost more for postal employees to count the words than the amount the post office might have gained in added business. In fact, I suspect the Government was trying to wean the French from pinching centimes. It is not by holding down to five words a message to your loved ones that you achieve an expansive economy, the Government seemed to be saying.

It may be that all this has some relation to President de Gaulle's pitch for a return to the gold standard. It is widely agreed that this would mean a huge rise in the price of gold—and a corresponding drop in the price of goods for those who own gold. Now, nobody knows how much gold the French have squirreled away, but there are those who say they can match Fort Knox ingot for ingot, without turning all their mattresses inside out. Revalue the gold, turn the country into one great bargain sale (entrée libre, of course) and who knows? France may outspend America yet.

LA COURTOISIE FRANCAISE

Paris—June, 1964

Like Americans, the French have been doing a lot of gloomy soul-searching of late. A publisher accuses his compatriots—especially those dealing with the money-laden tourist—of being *grincheux*, or grumpy. On the other hand, a professor, crying alarm at the invasion of American materialism, boasts that the typical Frenchman, even the man who checks the gas meter, possesses an aristocratic spirituality unknown to his opposite number across the Atlantic. This American, residing in Paris, has been unable to ascertain the spirituality of his meter man, because the chap is whisked through the apartment house under the suspicious eye of Madame la Concierge, with not a chance to exchange a word, spiritual or otherwise.

Experience suggests, however, that the two qualities, surliness and spirituality, may not be so incompatible as they seem. In fact, many Frenchmen may be grinchy because they are

109

spiritual, and resent the advance of materialism.

This raises an even more startling hypothesis—the existence of a spiritual underground dedicated to defeat progress by sullen sabotage.

Such a hypothesis would go far to explain the behavior in France of modern laundry machinery, which elsewhere is effectively erasing the picturesque sight of kneeling maids scrubbing linen on the rocky banks of streams.

Here, the mangle really justifies its name. Given the French affinity for the play on words, and recalling the wartime Resistance, when German rocket bases were so often destroyed on the very day they were completed, can anyone be sure that an anti-materialistic underground is not at work?

Further evidence comes to hand at every side. A recent arrival here entered the rental salon of a leading piano manufacturer and announced his interest in leasing an instrument. The department head, a lady of a certain age, coldly inquired, "Do you live in a furnished or unfurnished apartment?" Caught off balance, the would-be customer stammered, "Furnished." Triumphantly, the manageress retorted, "We do not rent to furnished apartments," and turned away. The man said, "But my office can furnish references . . ." She turned, eyebrows raised, "Is it your office that wants to rent a piano?" She did not wait for an answer. Another blow for the underground?

The hypothesis goes far to explain a number of irritants in everyday life in France—the cabbie at the taxi stand who is never going your way, the 20-minute wait to cash a check at your own bank, while half a dozen clerks slowly pass it from hand to hand, and all the grinchiness one may encounter. Frenchmen interviewed on the subject all said, in one way or another, "You mustn't think that this surliness is aimed only at foreigners. 'They' treat 'us' the same way."

"All this has happened since the war," one Parisian said, echoing a common refrain. "The

Occupation did something to us. Before, there was such a thing as *courtoisie Française*."

Actually, the Parisian himself was the soul of courtesy, as are many others one encounters at all social levels, including the cabbie who, the other day, ran after an American with a 50-franc note the passenger had given him in mistake for 10. It was an act of gross materialism, God bless him.

SOPHISTICATED SIN

Paris—November, 1965

[In a misguided effort to persuade Americans to spend their money at home in 1965, Senator Fulbright urged that they shun this sinkhole in favor of New Orleans or Las Vegas, "at least for a year or so." His speech delighted the Paris press.]

Senator Fulbright's blast at the "sophisticated debauchery" of Paris has proved balm to the French ego and may prove a boon to tourism, but it has baffled the foreign community here. Sophisticated? Debauchery? Some of the Senator's colleagues, examining the world situation on counterpart funds, may have discovered suave excesses unknown to Arkansas. But perhaps, in the haste of their passage, they received a wrong impression.

Take kissing. A recent study finds that the typical French couple are affianced for 22 months before they become m'sieur'dame. Where do they spend that interminable engagement? Together, of course, close together—but in the most public places they can find. At a sidewalk café, the sitters watch the passersby, the passersby stare at the sitters, but nobody wastes a glance at Jean and Marie, wound in a blind embrace at an outside table. In a bistro crowded at lunchtime, Jean and Marie nibble alternately at their sandwiches and at each other. Nobody pays any mind. Imprisoned with other pedestrians on a traffic island in a swarming boulevard, they seal off the noise and fumes with a kiss, until the light changes. Not a motorist sounds a derisive horn.

Going home in the Metro, seated knee to knee with strangers, they chat about the doings in the office and, in pauses, fall into a passionate clinch, again apparently ignoring, and being ignored by, their neighbors. A thought occurs, contact is broken, one of them speaks, the other replies, they clinch again. Often, Marie's sister Irene tags along. The three were observed the other day "doing" a local museum. Jean and Marie stop before the first exhibit, and find each other's lips. Irene carefully studies another showcase. Jean and Marie break and study exhibit. Irene joins them. They discuss exhibit. Jean and Marie move on to Exhibit 2 (and embrace), while Irene goes to No. 3). . . . And so it went. Irene seemed to find it all most educational. Observe Jean and Marie strolling in the park at nightfall. Do they seek out a secluded spot? Not at all. They walk hand in

112

hand through the dark places under the trees, and pause under the lamp posts to smooch.

What impresses one foreign resident, finally, is the innocence of it all. The 22-month public embrace comes to seem less a private exploration than a kind of secular publication of the banns, a prolonged, more or less animated, engagement announcement. "Look," Marie seems to be saying, "I've got my man." "Look," Jean avows, "I've got my girl."

The foreigner was more intrigued than annoyed one day when he missed a Metro train because such a couple was blocking the gate. He asked a young married Parisian, who had been through it all not long ago, what it was all about. The young man looked surprised.

"*Mais, c'est normale!*" he said.

The visitor persisted. Why, he asked, did couples at the movies wait for the intermission lights to go on before falling into a clinch?

The young man looked as though the visitor had lost his wits. He shook his head and then demanded, "Would you want them to miss the film?"

THE CROWDED BAR

When Monsieur X, the French equivalent for John Doe, needs legal help, he has an *embarras de choix*. He may employ an *avocat*, an *avoué*, an *agréé*, a *conseiller juridique*, a *notaire*, or a *société fiduciaire*. If he's litigious, or just very active, it's quite possible that he will need all of them.

Now, therefore, be it known that the Minister of Justice, René Pleven, Keeper of the Seals, deposed a bill to simplify the problem—to wit, by merging the first three professions aforementioned and by praying that the fourth will eventually just fade away. But as might be imagined, the parties of the first, second, and

114

third part, not to mention the fourth, are far from agreed on what would serve the best interest of their collective client, Monsieur X.

The three occupations whose merger is contemplated comprise what may be called the uniformed branch of the legal profession. The avocat in court wears a black robe and white dickie with a black epitoge, or rudimentary cloak, carried dashingly over the left shoulder. The avoué carries the same costume, minus the epitoge. The agréé sports a kind of morning coat and gray trousers, like the father of the bride.

Roughly speaking, the 7000 avocats are like English barristers, their main function being to plead in court. The avoués, limited to about 1500 in number, are filers of briefs (sometimes prepared by others but necessarily signed by an avoué); one can become an avoué only by inheriting the post or buying it. The agréés, fewer than 30 now, plead only before certain commercial tribunals. Like the avoués, their function is virtually hereditary, dating from an epoch when no self-respecting avocat would handle a trade dispute. Not involved in the proposed reform are the notaires, who handle property transactions and hence wills and marriage contracts, nor the fiduciaires, who specialize in tax matters.

All these specialized professions, which have grown up over the centuries, skirt the field of advice to citizens not yet caught in the toils of justice, or of marriage, death, and taxes—what might be called preventive law. This gap has been filled by the conseiller juridique. The function is scarcely defined by law and anybody can practice it, even an exconvict—or a foreigner. But the complexities of modern business life have caused many companies to turn to conseillers juridiques for advice on contracts, mergers, and so on, and often to put them on the payroll—a situation forbidden to any member of the approved professions.

The driving force behind the reform movement has been the National Association of Avocats and particularly its younger and hungrier members, who regard the unregulated and growing ranks of legal advisers with deep disapproval. To their disappointment, Minister Pleven rejected their proposal to outlaw the conseiller juridique. He did, however, propose to merge the avoués and agréés into the avocats, creating a profession more comparable to that of the American lawyer. The obsolete avoués and agréés would be compensated for the loss of their monopolies through surcharges on court fees.

Many members of all three professions turned out, nevertheless, to be firmly opposed to fiddling with traditions. The dissenting National Union of Avocats argued that a bill purporting to improve the lot of the clients would actually impose upon them the cost of buying out the avoués. Many critics charged that the reformers were unjust to French justice, whose chief problem, they held, was budgetary—not enough judges and not enough facilities for them. Among the critics was Aram Kevorkian, a former Philadelphia and New York lawyer who is one of the leading conseillers juridiques of Paris. "These young avocats are talking about a 'new man' who can do everything, at a time when people in all professions are specializing," he said in an interview. "In the American system, some people only argue cases, some only write briefs, some do nothing but corporate law, some handle only accidents. One result is the gigantism of American law firms. And the fees are considerably higher.

"The French system is built-in specialization. The young man decides in advance to make his career by filing briefs, or arguing in court, or writing mortgages and wills, or being a judge. The conseiller juridique, who may not do any of those things, ends up doing what a lawyer really should be doing—giving advice. The French lawyer can

115

charge less partly because he puts on less razzle-dazzle. How many American lawyers conduct their business from their living rooms?"

Mr. Kevorkian said the individualism of the French would in any case inhibit any grouping of legal services. "Just as he puts a wall around his house," the lawyer explained, "the French bourgeois doesn't want a lot of people to know his business." If they had their way, he opined, the young reformers would be disappointed in their hopes of acquiring quickly the business now going to their elders.

"They blame the system," he said, "when it's just the nature of the society."

THE PAPER CHASE

Paris–December, 1964

An abstract impressionist named Bertrand Dorny found himself caught recently in a plight that was all too realistic. He was driving back to Paris from Luxembourg one morning in a cheerful frame of mind, having had what he called a "not bad" reception at an exhibition there, and having sold several pictures. At the border, the Luxembourg guards waved him on without a glance at the remaining paintings, stacked on the roof of his Deux Chevaux. Two hundred meters farther on, the French customs guards stopped him and demanded an import permit. Thunderstruck, Mr. Dorny exclaimed that the pictures were domestic products, having been painted in Paris by a Frenchman. The guards were unmoved: no paper, no entry. Finally, Mr. Dorny turned back. But when he reached the Luxembourg post, the guards stopped him—and demanded an import permit.

Mr. Dorny showed them the letter of invitation to the exhibition, which had admitted the pictures the first time. But the guards pointed out that the show was over. For hours, Mr. Dorny bounced between the customs posts like a shuttlecock, pleading, cajoling, shouting. He began to think he was doomed, like some character in Kafka, to an unending traversal of a bureaucratic no man's land.

Finally, one of the Luxembourgeois relented enough to put the artist in touch by telephone with a sympathetic local merchant, who arrived after dark with appropriate forms and arranged to import the paintings a few meters into Luxembourg and then export them, properly stamped, to their native land.

The affair was a fair example of the love–hate relationship between the French and the *fiche*, or paper form—love, on the part of the state's innumerable employees, and hate, on the part of the rest of the population. Hate often yields to resignation. In a Paris commissariat not long ago, an elderly man was standing in a queue with a bulging knapsack under his shoulder. When his turn came, he emptied the knapsack's load of

116

papers on the counter. From a distance, one could observe, as in pantomime, the clerk ask for another document. Without a word, the man stuffed all his papers back in the knapsack, hoisted it, and shuffled away, looking as though he hadn't expected to get his fiche stamped that day anyhow.

There are those who say bureaucracy is more mechanized in the United States, more rigid in Germany, and more irrational in Italy. Still, it seems doubtful that these can surpass the French in ingenuity.

Social welfare is said to account for one-sixth of the national income, but a large portion of this must be consumed by the army of employees that thinks up the regulations and applies them. And this figure of one-sixth cannot include the outlay of unpaid time such as was to be seen the other afternoon at the Gare St. Lazare, where a long queue waited ten minutes while a young man

proved to the satisfaction of an agent that he was a member of a *famille nombreuse*, and so entitled to a discount on a second-class ticket to a suburb (regular roundtrip fare 1.5 francs).

The prudent resident always carries, if not a knapsack, at least a wallet full of documents. You never know when you may need them. A case in point was last year's Dassault affair. Two rural policemen were making a routine check when they stumbled on the lonely farmhouse where kidnappers were holding, under careless guard, the wife of one of France's leading industrialists. The woman, whose picture had been on all the front pages for days, cried, "I am Madame Dassault."

At this moment, the nation's acclaim was awaiting the two gendarmes. But bitter laughter greeted them instead, for, true to his training, the elder policeman replied to the lady, "Where are your papers?"

POMPIDOUISTE?

Paris—June, 1969

The election of Georges Pompidou as President provoked a grave debate among experts on the French language, who in this country alone number 50 million. *Qu'est-ce-que c'est le derivatif de Pompidou?* In other words, how do you label a follower of the man, and what adjective do you use to denote his style or policy?

The question might normally be settled by the high court of appeal on the language, the French

Academy. In the eternal, Sisyphean labor of bringing its dictionary up to date, the 40 Immortals are midway through the letter C and, with all deliberate speed, should reach the Ps in 10 or 15 years.

However, a functionary remarked with evident relief that the academicians had recently reaffirmed an ancient decision to keep proper names and their derivatives out of the Book. This will spare them the risk of appearing to enter the political arena when they get to the Gs a few years from now. For the public, anyhow, that problem has long been settled, with Gaulliste in general use—although fancy writers occasionally indulge in Gaullien to denote the style of the man, with perhaps a soupçon of irony.

Professor Robert Escarpit of the University of Bordeaux, a linguist who is also a noted satirist (the combination is not exceptional here), once suggested that the success of Charles de Gaulle in becoming the incarnation of France might be due partly to his parents, who endowed him with the name of the game. "Just suppose he was named Bertrandinet des Aygigulfes, Sigismond de Troule-Huc, or simply Martin," Professor Escarpit wrote. "His appeal of June 18 [1940] would have fallen flat."

On the other hand, another Gaul survived, in history if not on the battlefield, despite the name Vercingetorix.

When the General plucked Georges Pompidou out of obscurity to become his Premier in 1962, critics leaped on the name as intrinsically comic, like the sound of Mr. Pompidou's birthplace, Montboudif, which has a ring like Keokuk to French ears. But as *Le Figaro* recalled the other day, Mr. Pompidou had the last laugh. The derisive nickname Pompon turned out to have an affectionate overtone, like Popeye, poupée (doll), or papa. Gibes about Mr. Pompidou's native Auvergne also boomeranged. The Auvergnat, like the Scot, is a jokebook symbol for thrift, slyness, and stubbornness, but the French, like the Britons, sometimes decide that those are desirable qualities for a statesman.

Adding a syllable or two to Pompidou poses a difficult decision. A few journalists have accepted the obvious solution, Pompidouiste. To pronounce it requires a pause between "ou" and "iste" and as Professor Escarpit observed in his column in *Le Monde* the other day, "the French cannot stand the hiatus." The more common resort has been to Pompidoliste or Pompidolien, which have been in use since it became clear that the former Premier was a political force in his own right—that is, since General de Gaulle promoted him into "the national reserve" a year ago and Mr. Pompidou began showing signs of impatience to claim the succession.

The objection to the solution in "liste" and even more in "lien" is that, as one good linguist pointed out in an interview, they sound "a bit frivolous, if not humorous," for application to the occupant of the Elysée Palace (an Elyséen, of course).

119

Learned authorities have also argued that, by analogy with other names from the south of France, proper usage demands Pompidoriste or Pompidorien. Equally learned authorities have riposted with Latin and Greek derivations, such as "dulcien." The advocates of Pompidou-Pompidoliste cite analogy with *fou* (mad) and its feminine form, *folle*, and *mou-molle* (soft).

"All this is a bit of fantasy," the linguist said. "It is fake etymology. There is no rule. In a case like this a word arises spontaneously, from the first person who writes it."

French is rich in inventions to meet problems such as what to call a man from Michigan. Thus Strasbourg is inhabited by Strasbourgeois, Bordeaux by Bordelais, Limoges by Limousins, St. Cloud by Clodoaldiens, Puteaux by Putéoliens, St.-Dié by Déodatiens, St.-Denis by Dionysiens, Nice by Niçois, Besançon by Bisontins, Cahors by Cadurciens, Pau by Palois, Dax by Dacquois, Béziers by Bitterois, Malakoff by Malakoffiots, Fontainebleau by Bellifontains, Montelimar by Montiliens, St.-Malo by Malouins, Bourges by Berruyters, Evreux by Ebroiciens, and so on.

Mr. Pompidou married a Castrogontérienne— that is, a girl from Château-Gontier. French is, as everyone knows, the language of logic par excellence.

Derivations of proper names tend to take "-iste" or "-ien" or "-in," or the pejorative "-ard," as in Dreyfusard—which ultimately became a badge of honor. But French grammar, sacred as it is, must yield to French wit or elegance. So fans of the playwright-novelist Jean Giraudoux are pleased to be called Giralduciens.

Some admirers of the new President have proposed Pompidoué, the word "doue," meaning gifted. Less flattering suggestions include Pompidolé, implying sorrow; Pompidoll, an allusion in Franglais to the President's once-reputed preference for the company of show people; Pompidourrière, suggesting a reactionary or a grandmother, and, should it come to that, Pompidolâtre, implying adulation.

Professor Escarpit, seeking a consonant to break up the hiatus, toyed with Pompidoviste, but discarded it as smelling of Bolshevism. Another linguist came up with a coinage more promising for French-American relations: Pompidollar. Whether the successor to Gaullism—whatever comes to be its accepted name—will go that far remains to be seen.

THE INVISIBLE RACE

Paris—August, 1966

From a reporter's point of view, the most intriguing thing about the biking marathon called the Tour de France is that it's invisible. I don't suppose any other sporting event is less seen by more spectators. Perhaps 10 million fans this year lined 2641 miles of road looping around France and corners of neighboring countries. After waiting for hours in rain, subtropical heat, or Alpine snow, what did they see? A daylong parade of weird vehicles peddling bugkiller, pop singers, scotch tape and liver paste, and in the middle a scrawny, sweaty platoon of bikers pedaling by in a matter of seconds. Hardly time enough to read the ads on their shirts. This is a sporting contest? Well, yes, and quite a dramatic one. But try and cover it.

The couple of hundred reporters who do try every year are hardly better off than the spectators. Driving on the narrow roads, they must keep either well ahead of or well behind the racing pack. From time to time, an official car radios them the positions of the riders. Rarely, on a broad stretch, the judges may wave a few press cars past the pack, to get a glimpse of the open-mouthed heroes.

This is hard for a newsman to admit, but a hats-off exception has got to be made here for half a dozen cameramen. They do get to see the race, at a price. They spend the 22 days, rain or shine, mounted tandem on motorcycles, weaving around the pack, often plunging down steep grades and around hairpin turns, facing backward with both hands holding their cameras, grinding away. Every one of them old enough to know better, too. Too bad they can't write.

As a matter of fact, taking notes in a car doing racing skids every 20 seconds or so while falling down a mountain is not very practical, either. But it's not necessary. After 53 years, the Tour has become a marvel of organization. Within an hour of the finish each day, a mobile computer has ground out a complete statistical report and a running account of the race. All the journalists have to do is shake well and add a little coloring.

"Before television," said a Belgian newsman mournfully, "we could really write up a storm."

As it happened, I ran into some undeserved luck. Sent down to take a peek at the Tour as it pushed into the Alps, I had to beg transportation, and as the only American in the press corps and hence an exotic creature, I was allowed to spend my first day in the judge's car accompanying the lead bikers. This day saw a gallant effort by a world champion to prove his title on a terrible climb, only to be overtaken, and, after a long and agonizing duel, to fall back beaten. By the finish I was hooked. I had to see how this would come out, at least through the Alps. I had left my passport in Paris, but during the next three days I sailed grandly across the Italian, Swiss, and French frontiers with hardly a glance at the saluting border guards.

Filing stories was a little harder. In Briançon, after an hour's wait, I got Paris on the line and began dictating the deathless drama related above, not sparing the wordage. After saying "finis" I waited, and learned I had been talking into a dead phone all the while. . . . In Turin, the press room of the new concrete stadium has a glass wall facing south, forming a solar cooker.

121

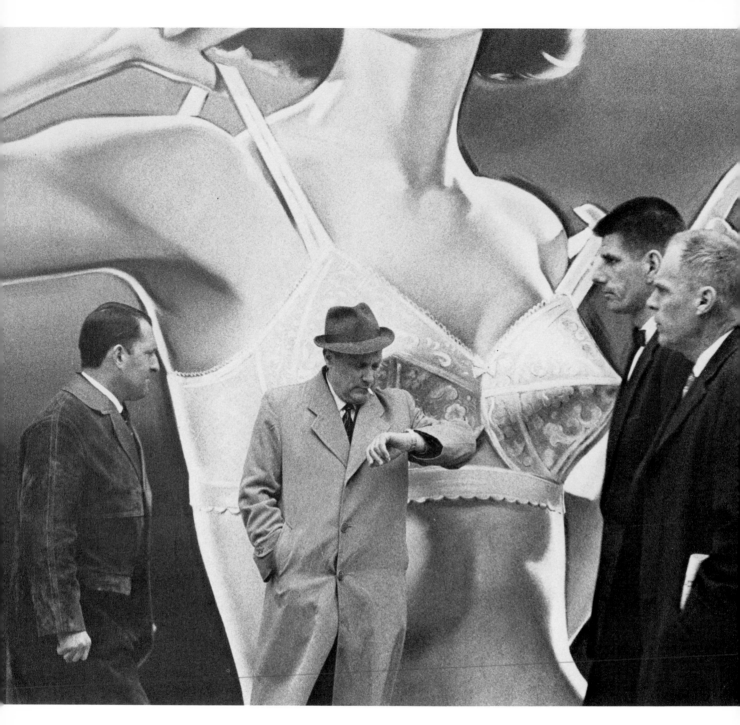

122

The sight of 200 ill-conditioned, middle-aged journalists stripped to the waist and snarling as they pecked at their portables was a memorable one. The phone booth was an oven inside an oven, and it was necessary to close the door against the racket.

Briançon—July, 1966

This was the day the old pros set out to take the Tour de France away from the young pros. It was the most punishing day of what may be the most exhausting ordeal that goes by the name of a sporting contest, and for an hour and 20 minutes, it was also Tom Simpson's day. At the age of 28, Simpson is one of the old pros. A sunken-cheeked, hawk-nosed Englishman, he is the world champion of bike racing.

Before today's run of 95 miles over the steepest mountains of the 2641-mile Tour, Simpson wearily summed up the situation. After fifteen racing days, with seven to go, the old stars now found themselves about seven minutes behind a group of young upstarts. The main reason was a feud between Jacques Anquetil, five-time winner of the Tour, and Raymond Poulidor. For the first week, each sullenly waited for the other to break out and set a pace. The other old pros waited, too. "The first day in the Pyrenees," Simpson said, "we all looked at each other. We were eight minutes back. Now we're slowly whittling the lead down, but it's a hell of a job."

Simpson explained that the smaller men, and above all the Spaniards, were great in the mountains. On a steep climb they gear down, pedal fast, and stay ahead. "It's a question of rhythm," he said. "I've got to keep my gear turning steadily. If I shifted to the low gear, I'd have to pedal fast, I'd lose oxygen, get asphyxiated."

The Tour de France is a moving circus about one hundred miles long, all honky-tonk except for the band of sallow heroes in the middle. And they wear the colors of the seven companies that pay them. This morning, as any other, the vehicles plugging pop singers and aerosol bombs and other commercial products went on ahead from Bourg-d'Oisans. Then at 11 A.M., the pack set out, 116 strong, through the sunny Alpine valley, with white torrents roaring down the mountainsides from the melting snows. Within 15 minutes, a Ford rider had tumbled on a turn and was up and off again rubbing his wrists. Then began a climb of 4280 feet in 14 miles to the Croix de Fer, peak of the Iron Cross. The pack slowly disintegrated as the riders, dripping sweat, their mouths open, gasping for the thin mountain air, toiled uphill at 5 miles an hour.

The narrow road suddenly dipped and the pack hit 25 m.p.h. around the bends into a tunnel carved through snow. Great herds of sheep grazed in the green valleys, ignoring the strange caravan. At 12:23 P.M., with a clump of Spaniards in the lead, the pack reached the Iron Cross and then spilled down a steep hairpin road. At up to 50 m.p.h. it was a terrifying ride even for the escort cars, skidding on the turns overhanging the precipice. Simpson fell, got first aid, and was off with new patches on a leg and forearm.

At the bottom, the pack slowed to 30 m.p.h. to pass through the town of St. Michel de Maurienne, where they snatched lunch sacks and rolled on. A medic leaning from a convertible dabbed cotton at a gash on a rider's leg. The rider

123

did not miss a stroke. The grade began to climb and suddenly there was Simpson out ahead of the pack, plugging steadily, his mouth open, a faraway look in his blue eyes. For half an hour, he was out there all alone. Along the road, where clumps of watchers had been huddling since dawn for a glimpse of the Tour, the word passed like magic. It was "Allez Simpson" all the way.

Then out of nowhere came a small Ford rider. It was Julio Jimenez, a 32-year-old Spanish mountain champion. He caught up as if Simpson were standing still. The two stuck together in slow motion uphill, now side by side, now one leading. Jimenez pedaled furiously in low gear while Simpson pumped steadily, took shelter behind the other when he could, picked up a little on the curves. The pair passed Telegraph Hill, shot down, and then started up the toughest slope of all to Galibier Pass, highest in the Tour de France. The road there is 8307 feet high. Two miles from

the top, Simpson faltered and Jimenez seemed to take off. By this time, somehow the word seemed to have passed to the thin, shivering line of fans. They were cheering Jimenez. "Allez hombre," a man cried. Simpson disappeared into the pack where Poulidor and Anquetil were making their belated push.

Jimenez incredibly kept far in the lead up to the cloudy peak, past a glacier and down into the green valley to the finish line of the day. As the first to Balibier, he won $2,000.

Two-and-a-half minutes behind came Anquetil, barely ahead of Poulidor. The two had picked up four minutes on the leaders of the Tour and were back in strong contention. In eighteenth place came Tom Simpson, bleeding profusely from a gash in his elbow. He had brushed against a motorcycle on the descent and fallen again. Nobody cheered. He was awarded a prize for the unluckiest rider of the day.

Turin, Italy—July, 1966

The Tour de France began a loop through the Italian Alps on a note of high drama and ended the act on a note of comic opera. To play the film backward, the Belgian, Herman van Springel, pulled away flying in the last mile of a grueling 100-mile ride, only to be steered by a cop into a parking lot at the stadium entrance. By the time he managed to unscramble from the friendly crowd and find the finish line, he was in fifth place for the day. First in was one of the few Italians in the race, Franco Bitossi, who is twenty-first in the general standings.

The drama really began at noon in Briançon, France, when the world champion, Tom Simpson, insisted on starting against a physician's orders.

He had five new stitches in his elbow and was in obvious pain. He set out gamely holding the right handlebar between thumb and forefinger. He stayed with the pack halfway up the first mountain. Then he slipped back, way back. A doctor pulled up alongside but Simpson shook him off. He plugged away to the top, past the Italian frontier, and skimmed down at 45 miles an hour. Simpson seemed to be gaining speed when he waved his throbbing arm and pulled up. The race was over for him.

On the same descent Guido de Rosso had a bad spill and was hospitalized. This did not seem to dampen the enthusiasm of the countryside. All of the northwest Italians seemed to be lining the hilly route, smiling, cheering, and spraying the panting cyclists with cool water from bottles, pails, and hoses. This was usually welcome in the savage July heat, but not always.

Occasionally an enthusiast would give a friendly shove to a hard-working rider. This meant a fine to the rider if a judge observed it, even though it was assumed he was innocent.

The lead in the general standings was taken by Lucien Aimar of France, a Ford teammate of Anquetil's. The strength of the Ford team has caused some muttering among French followers of the race, especially after Ford's victory at Le Mans. They point out that Ford doesn't even build cars in France. But it's a funny race. One team wears the Rising Sun emblem of a Japanese washing machine.

Turin—July, 1966

With the bicycle riders in the Tour de France resting here before heading for home through the Great Saint Bernard Pass tomorrow, nobody is saying the nasty word "doping" any more. Yet the race this year has made history in the field of hopped-up athletics. It marked the first effort of France to enforce her new law making it a crime to induce a contender to better effort by certain biochemical means. And it saw the first strike of professional athletes in defense of the needle.

The affair began in Bordeaux following the eighth day of the 22-day grind when gendarmes and physicians in the pay of the Sports Ministry burst into boudoirs for a random sampling of bikers. The physicians demanded and obtained urine specimens from a score of athletes while the lawmen went through their baggage. French policemen can be charming in giving directions to the ladies, but they are sometimes impulsive in other duties. The following day in the foothills of the Pyrenees, the racing pack suddenly dismounted and silently walked 100 yards or so pushing the bicycles. Having made their point, they remounted and headed for the hills.

Nobody denied that the riders were getting synthetic help. "But why pick on us?" they demanded. Why not, they asked, go after the student taking benzedrine before an exam or the businessman gulping tranquilizers? Why not go after amateur athletes? The immediate answer was that enforcement had to begin somewhere, that the cyclists' use of the needle was notorious and that the Tour de France was a conspicuous place for the authorities to tell the sports world they meant business.

But the stoppage seems to have worked. There have been no more inspections and the results of the Bordeaux analyses have not been announced. The guess among cynical writers here is that they never will be.

The feeling is that an antidrugging law may be unenforceable. The big problem is how to define drugging. In justifying himself, Tom Simpson touched on this point. "When you get up in the morning," he asked, "do you need a cup of coffee to get started? Well, after doing 150 miles the day before, we might need three or four coffees."

In the race, riders carry flasks of coffee, packets of sugar, and other fortifying things. Nobody questions their right to all the carbohydrates, proteins, minerals, and vitamins they need. When they are in pain, which is often, nobody can

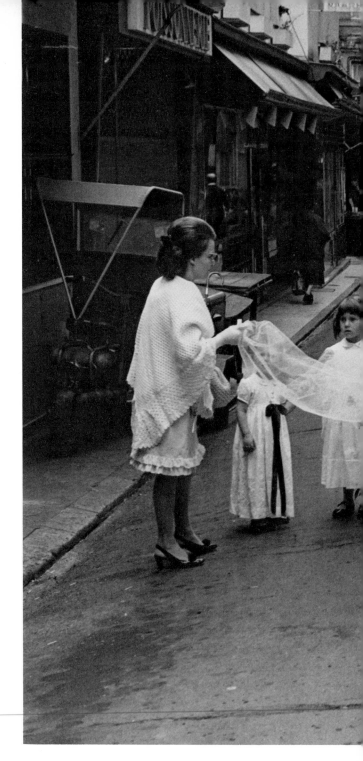

question their right to sedation. But some pain-killers, tranquilizers, caffeine, and vitamins in certain doses can spur a man or a horse to go faster than he normally would. The trainers, with or without medical degrees, all are supposed to have their personal recipes. "My man knows what's good for me," the star said.

There is the rub, in the view of the authorities. The doses administered in tough competition may be good for the performance; they are not good for the performers. It is widely believed that many bad spills are caused by over-drugged riders. And nobody could call the wan, skinny heroes of this race a picture of health. How can society protect the athletes against themselves? Judging from the Tour de France, the answer has not been found.

Paris—July, 1966

Jacques Anquetil, the nonpareil of bicycle racing, abandoned the Tour de France on the home stretch. Wracked by chill and fever, and soaked by a 138-mile mountain ride through a cold rain, the skinny blond Norman dismounted and said, "I'm finished." It may well have been his last race.

Anquetil had won the Tour de France five times, more than any other rider. At 32 years of age, he had not wanted to tackle the 2641-mile, 22-day grind, but had yielded to urging from the fans. Ironically, the end came at the foot of a hill much smaller than many that the 83 surviving riders had climbed in their 19-day swing through the Pyrenees and Alps.

The day's 165-mile lap began in Chamonix under Mont Blanc and ended at St. Etienne. Anquetil, in eighth place, had worn himself out yesterday while sheltering and encouraging his teammate, Lucien Aimar, who had unexpectedly taken the lead in the over-all standing, but was having trouble on the slopes. The champion kept up with the pack for nearly half of today's ride, the longest of the tour. Then he slipped to the rear. Two teammates joined him and formed a windbreak, drawing him back to the pack. Twice more he made it and twice he fell back. Finally, as the pack began to climb a hill near the Rhône River, Anquetil pulled up and dismounted. "It's no use my going on, for as soon as it's uphill, I can't breathe any more. It's too bad I can't lend Aimar a hand any more. But really, I'm finished."

Anquetil said he had taken a chill yesterday from the soaking he had received from friendly spectators. All through Italy fans had doused the riders with water to cool them off. This was welcome going uphill, but the aftereffect was not so pleasant on the 50-mile-an-hour plunge down from the snows of Great Saint Bernard Peak.

On an earpopping descent in the Alps in the Tour de France, a top rider took a tumble. His injuries were minor but his bike was a wreck. In a flash, a teammate pulled up, handed him his own bike and waited for a truck to come with a spare. A little later another star, at a word from his manager, gave up his own lead position to fall back to the side of a faltering teammate. And throughout the 22-day ordeal, whenever a rider had a flat, two or three teammates would peel off from the pack and wait for the wheel change. Then, taking turns at forming a windscreen, the little group would weave its way single file back to the pack. It was a pretty sight and, to the uninformed, a baffling one.

What makes a bike rider pedaling his heart out for fame and fortune sacrifice his chances for a comrade, and this in a race scored on individual performance?

Money.

The curious economics of professional bike racing makes teamwork pay. There were signs in this Tour de France, however, that this system was breaking down and that a change may be in the making.

Each of the 130 riders who entered the 2,641-mile grind was a moving billboard. His shirt, his pants, his cap, and his bike bore the names of up to a dozen products. In advance of the pack went the floats of a hundred more advertisers. One sponsor estimated that 12 million spectators watched the ads go by, not to mention the television audiences of western Europe. With "exposure" like this, it is no mystery why Ford, which has nothing to do with bicycles, picked up the tabs for a team of hungry riders. At the finish, where a Ford rider came in first, a crude sign pointed up the message: "One more reason Ford is the best."

The winner, Lucien Aimar, did not touch a sou of the prize money. That's a Tour de France tradition and it's perfectly sensible. In the stadium paddock, where the riders were cooling off and promoters were trotting around with fountain pens at the ready, Aimar signed contracts for exhibition races estimated to earn him $12,000 in the next five weeks. His prize money for the Tour de France was a nice inducement to his teammates, and well earned.

Aside from the big winner, all riders share equally in the total winnings of each team—prizes offered by commercial sponsors for each lap, for tough hills, for hard luck, for the gamest smile, and so forth. Shares ranged from $300 to $1,600. But the real inducement for individual effort was the size of the "starting money" that promoters would offer a rider to take part in future races.

The curious psychology of the road racer helps promote teamwork. It is well established that a racer can go faster—afoot, on a bike, or in a car—with a competitor in front of him, and not only because of the vacuum effect. Riders agree that they do better with a teammate alongside, and tend to get demoralized if every time they put on an extra burst they find a stubborn competitor staying with them. So in bike racing, a team will send weaker riders ahead to dog the opposition or to lure an opposing champion into exceeding his strength. It is permitted also to block the opposition. But it is not permitted for two or more teams to combine. Just such a gangup was alleged to have occurred in the final laps of the Tour de France. With important contracts to be distributed at the end, there was talk of a combine in favor of the forerunner and against the No. 2 and No. 3 riders. A German contender was publicly warned, and judges on motorcycles policed the last 200 miles, but nothing was proved.

In an angry editorial after the finish, Jacques Godet, the editor of the sporting newspaper *L'Equipe* and boss of the tour, attributed unspecified "misdeeds" to "the very nature of the system that accentuates more and more a certain form of corruption, the introduction of habits born of submission to financial interests." Godet said changes would be made next year.

130

This would not imply taking the cash out of racing, which would horrify even such a competitive pro as Tom Simpson, the world champion. Simpson came to Paris in civvies to collect the hard-luck prize of the Tour de France. He took it with his left hand, his right being still all but helpless as a result of the terrible fall that put him out of the race. But he planned to ride in a 62-mile race in Belgium the next day. Told this was madness, he retorted in his broad North-of-England accent, "A family moost eat, moostn't it?"

Actually, he acknowledged, a champion may earn up to £50,000 ($140,000) a year, riding as many as 200 days. "The hardest part is not the cycling," Simpson said. "It's the traveling. Riding, it's not disagreeable. Most bike riders—99 percent of the professionals—come from very working-class families, and might be lacking a bit of education. My father was a miner. Two of my teammates are miners' sons too, and the rest are from peasant families. Cycle sport is the only way they might make a comfortable living. A majority of riders say they'd never want their son to ride. I wonder. I had £10 ($280) when I went professional eight years ago. Now I've just finished a block of eight luxury flats, I've a car, my wife has a car. My people never knew what a holiday was. Now every winter we go for two months. I wouldn't change it."

[A year later, in another Tour de France, Tom Simpson was pedaling up a steep slope from the Côte d'Azur under a scorching sun when he fell as though he had been struck. He had died, apparently in the saddle. It was the heat, the judges said. It was that, and the drugs, and Tom's conviction that, in return for the money and glory, an old champion could not let the fans down.]

HUNTING SEASON

Paris—September, 1966

The Prefect of Paris explained why he had declared the hunting season open in the city, where game is to be found only on the table and may be attacked only with knife and fork. It was, he said, to preserve the right of urbanites to dream.

Bernard Lafay, a Gaullist councilman from the brick barrens of the seventeenth Arrondissement, had addressed a formal question, in writing, to Prefect Maurice Grimaud. Why, he demanded, did the list of departments where the game season opened include Paris, where shooting, trapping, or even chasing game with dogs is forbidden? Mr. Grimaud's reply, also formal, was made public today.

"It is well known," he wrote, "that the pleasure of hunting is quite distinct from that of shooting at game. . . . The Prefect of Police did not want to deprive Parisians of that portion of dream so essential to urban civilizations.

"It seemed to him that not to open the hunting season in Paris on the pretext that there is no game would be a little as if one gave up celebrating Christmas because there was not enough snow to go by sleigh to Midnight Mass."

He preferred to believe, he said, that as a result of the opening of the season, "more than one Parisian betook himself to work a little less morosely, dreaming past the subway construction sites of plowland and forest trails, and taking the first traffic policeman encountered in the morning fog to be some friendly gamekeeper."

Wild partridge, hare, rabbit, and quail returned to Paris restaurant larders almost immediately and waiters and clients swapped lies about their Sunday's shooting. It was the start of another hunting season in northern France, part commerce and part national passion. This year, the season was preceded by loud cries of alarm. A record total of two million citizens had paid $8 each for hunting licenses and a couple of dollars more for compulsory insurance against their shooting one another. But there was no compulsory supply of game. In fact, many neophytes were surprised to learn that their licenses did not even guarantee them access to a place to look for game. In Parliament, the people's representatives warned that there would not be enough game to go around.

There never is. Actually, a visit to one hunt on opening day and reports from others indicate that the season will be no worse than others in recent years, and perhaps better than average in the total kill. But there will also doubtless be more disappointed hunters than ever before. Hunting the whole is often smaller than the sum of its parts. For example, a poll of 24 shooters who crossed a field near Fontenay-Tésigny found they had downed an average of 2.3 partridges each.

The total bag was 15. This phenomenon is not unknown in the United States, but in other respects hunting here is strikingly different.

Game here has always been regarded as belonging to the land that nourishes it. When the land belonged to the nobility, no commoner could legally hunt; after the French Revolution, the right passed to the new owners. These in turn have over the years leased the better hunting rights to wealthy sportsmen, clubs, or corporations that stage hunts as fringe benefits for directors and important clients. The rent is traditionally expressed in hundredweight of wheat, presumed to be consumed by the game; it runs now to $6 or $7 an acre a year.

France offers good cover for game but also has an insatiable appetite for it. In addition to heavy hunting, recent years have produced new menaces: the myxamitosis rabbit plague, insecticides, and even the sonic boom, which is said to crack eggs in nests. Still, the affluent society has brought an outpouring of men of modest means who have been able to buy a license and a gun but have no place to shoot. In the last three years, the Government has tried to meet the problem by encouraging the formation of community shooting societies, pooling communal lands with farms too small to be worth developing as private preserves. Dues are cheap, as low as three dollars a year. But game is scarce, too. More and more, the game is limited to those who can afford to stock it.

Jean Brueghel, a waiter in a café in the Latin Quarter, arose at five o'clock on his hunting day and drove 125 miles to a communal range near Auxerre, where he was a guest of his in-laws. He returned at midnight, emptyhanded. "I didn't even fire a shot," he said. The five hunters in his group all told bagged two hares, a rabbit, and a pigeon.

A vivid contrast was the hunt near Fontenay-Tésigny, 30 miles east of Paris. Here a dozen Paris businessmen grouped in the Amicale de

133

Boitron, each pay $1,000 to $1,200 a year to attend a hunt each week for twenty weeks. The dues are not unusually high; some clubs run to $4,000 a year. The Amicale's funds pay not only for hunting rights to its 3000 acres, but also for two gamekeepers and for raising and feeding game, primarily pheasants and hares.

In the simple stone lodge, Paul Goux, a machinery dealer and president of the Amicale, greeted the hunters with coffee, croissants, and a pleasant but firm lecture on safety. Minor violations cost a bottle of champagne, he said, major ones . . . He pursed his lips. Then he divided the hunters by lot into three teams, and led the procession to the first site, a fog-shrouded field of stubble and sugar beets. As always, the hunt began in a corner of the preserve so as to drive game away from the neighbors.

Guided by a hunting horn and a white flag, two teams in a skirmish line began converging from two sides toward the third, stationary line. Partridges could be heard chucking in the morning fog. From time to time a covey broke cover and guns cracked. Now and again a hare leaped up and dashed first toward one line, then to another. Some got away, some did not. Several

pheasants fled for the woods, unscathed; their season opens September 25. At the end, the teams moved to another site and switched roles. They stopped only for a French hunter's lunch at the lodge, a simple affair of calf's head, roast lamb with beans, salad, cheese, coffee, and four or five wines. Shooting resumed in the hot afternoon. Gathered again at dusk for champagne, they tallied the day's bag: 80 partridges, 29 hares, 3 pigeons, 1 quail, 4 larks. This tended to confirm a member's estimate that an average season would yield 1500 to 2000 kills.

Each day's take is equally divided among the hunter-members. Poorer clubs and communal societies let each hunter keep his kill. Larger operations, with uniformed beaters who drive the game to the seated hunters, keep the game for commercial sale. There is in any event much more game than those hunters could eat.

The problem is at the bottom of the scale, where there are more hunters than game. Mass affluence and leisure, and the effort of the Government to satisfy popular demand, is frightening the traditionalists. They fear that the Government may in the end take over hunting rights entirely.

HYSTERIA IN ORLEANS

Orléans–June, 1969

Jewish merchants of Orléans have been victims of a slander campaign recalling the Middle Ages and the Salem witch hunt. A rumor that the storekeepers were drugging and kidnapping women customers to sell them into white slavery arose apparently out of nowhere very recently. It swept this peaceful and prosperous region of 150,000 like wildfire. Alarmed liberals and merchants—most of them non-Jewish—published belated denials of the story. As of this writing the fever appeared to be abating. Yet interviews with shoppers, children, and elders demonstrated that the public still half believes the vicious scandal. It was notable that in the stores directly involved, female customers almost never entered alone. They came in threes, or accompanied by husbands, or not at all. "It was certainly not spontaneous," a high police official said. "I'm convinced it was organized."

The instigators appear to have obtained their raw material from a sex-and-crime weekly called *Noir et Blanc*. A month ago, under the caption "Kidnapping in Grenoble," it recounted the following tale: A man accompanied his wife to a garment store but waited outside for her. Impatient, he went inside, to be told that the woman had not been there. He never saw her again. Like many others, she had been spirited off to be sold to the brothels of the Middle East.

The story was of course totally fictitious, but about ten days after it was published, it reappeared here by word of mouth, with ugly embellishments. The rumor placed the incident in a neat, modern apparel store, Chez Dorphé, near the central market of Orléans. As in *Noir et Blanc*,

the husband was supposed to have gone to the police, but their search was now successful: They found the wife and two other women, drugged and bound, in the cellar. The story grew to include a tunnel to a nearby shoe store, and the tunnel grew to reach a popular apparel shop on a main street half a mile away, La Boutique de Sheila. Added details were an elevator that led to the tunnel, drug-tipped pins used for adjusting hems, brassieres with concealed needles, and so on. At least eight stores, all Jewish-owned, were mentioned as members of the ring. The rumor mongers anticipated the objection that nothing had appeared in the press. They said "Jewish Gold"—precisely ten million old francs, or $20,000—had been given to the police to be spread around to hush up the affair.

The victims learned about it just before the Pentecost weekend, May 25–27. Mrs. Jacqueline Llados, non-Jewish manager of a Jewish-owned store, said a friend came in and said, jestingly: "Don't you have a trapdoor here, at least?"

"I was born here, and I've never seen anything like it," she said. "Nothing ever happens in Orléans, except the Joan of Arc Festival. But people came by, nudging and pointing inside. They didn't show any hatred, only fear, and a desire to talk. Of course we were not the main victims. They were Dorphé's, Felix's, and Sheila's. But our business was catastrophic. One of our main customers is a girl's shelter. The girls come in and charge things. Well, that Saturday, a sister came from the shelter, settled their accounts, and told me I was not to serve any of their girls unless they came accompanied. None of them has come

135

since. We hardly ever see a woman come in alone. People say, 'There's no smoke without fire.'"

At a museum 100 yards away, a pleasant, middle-aged woman caretaker was asked what she thought. "Well," she replied, "There's no smoke without fire."

With the story now denied on all sides, would she go back to the stores in question?

"*Ma foi*," she replied, "I don't know. Yet they seemed nice . . ."

A pretty girl of about 20, walking home with a loaf of bread under her arm, declared: "I wouldn't go into a store alone . . . a cop warned me."

More disturbing to liberals here is the fact that a number of teachers in both the parochial and public schools appear to have uttered similar warnings to girl pupils. Maurice Rebaudet, a civil servant who is president of the high school

parents association, said, "The parents came to me absolutely terrified. They said they couldn't let their children out. The whole town was talking about it. I didn't believe the story, but my daughter did. So I decided it was my duty to do something, and I went to the police."

At headquarters he met the star victim of the hate campaign, a gentle, blue-eyed, 35-year-old man named Henri Light, manager of Dorphé's. Mr. Light had been living a nightmare and had decided to fight back. Trembling with anger, frustration and grief, he repeated his story in an interview yesterday.

"When people told me that Friday that I was dealing in drugs and women," he said, "I laughed. But when I got back, the town was enflamed. People crowded around the store outside, pointing. I felt like an animal exposed in a cage. I got phone calls, some humorous—like 'Send me a load of fresh meat'—and some enraged. My daughter Annie heard about it in school. In the Middle Ages, they accused us of stealing children to make matzoh. When they need a scapegoat, they attack the Jews. This is how it started in 1932, and it ended in the crematoriums. They let us alone for a while. Now it's starting again."

The victims, the authorities, and civic leaders faced a dilemma. To publicize the rumor, some feared, would only spread it. So for the first ten days or so, nothing was done. But the rumor grew. Mr. Light and five other merchants filed a complaint of slander against parties unknown, setting off a formal police investigation. Mr. Rebaudet of the Parents Association and two merchant organizations—few of whose members are Jewish—issued denunciations of the rumors as false and vicious. The two daily newspapers published these and added their own.

Perhaps most effective was a public meeting of notables called by Guy Brun, a young corporation executive, non-Jewish, who is president of the local League Against Racism and Anti-Semitism.

The League also filed a separate complaint, charging violation of the law against racist propaganda. Official and religious authorities, however, have so far held their silence on the affair—as have some of the victims—on the theory that it had best be allowed to die out.

Observers agree that the fever has dropped sharply since the denials began appearing. But a pretty 15-year-old, walking with two boys on a shopping street, nodded her blond head vigorously and said, "Oh, yes, there was this man waiting for his wife . . ."

A boy interrupted, "I don't believe it. I think somebody has it in for the owner. In my father's shop, this guy's wife disappeared, and it turned out she ran away with the bus driver." All three laughed.

At Sheila's, across the street, business was coming back, in twos and threes. Three factory girls, questioned, said they neither believed nor disbelieved the stories. "There's lots who believe it," one of them said defensively.

Mrs. Jeanette Buki, the dark, young-looking owner of the shop, said, with grief in her eyes, "Do you think I'd want to kidnap people?"

The first girl replied, "In appearance, no." The second said, "My mother says girls who disappear want to disappear." The third, "My mother says it's true." The second, reassuringly, "Anyhow, it's not this one, it's Dorphé's." The third girl, "I hear that it's all stores that have a given name, like Sheila, Felix . . ."

When a reporter objected, the first girl retorted, "Ah, but the police are in it, too."

Mrs. Buki said one of her own daughters had heard the story in school, the Lycée Jean Zay, a high school named for a French cabinet minister, a Jew, killed by the Nazis. An older daughter, coming home for Mother's Day, heard the "news" involving her mother from an old classmate on the train. "My children were overwhelmed," Mrs. Buki said. "I was tough. I said they'd have to

stand up to it. Maybe I did wrong? Now I wonder when the second wave will come. Maybe I'm pessimistic. I knew the war, I was seven, and people hid me. I didn't think it would happen here. I woke up different. I thought I was French, now I think I'm something else."

The police official, who asked that his name not be used, said none of the local "aristocracy" had ever believed the story, and that the public, which did, had at any rate never threatened violence. "If we were in the Middle Ages," he said, "the merchants would have been burned in the Place Jeanne D'Arc. But the people do not go into the stores," he added.

He indicated that the investigation would be a long and difficult one. Early efforts to track down the source of the rumor have run into general forgetfulness. Meanwhile, it will take a long time for the effects of the calumny to disappear.

"From now on," Mr. Rebaudet said sorrowfully, "Any girl who goes into one of those stores can't help thinking about it."

Said the policeman, "It just proves the stupidity of people."

Part Six **LA POLITIQUE**

A FEW NATIONAL CHARACTERISTICS

Paris—May, 1969

"You know as well as I do," said Georges Pompidou, "that the French are just about ungovernable."

The bitter but proud irony of the comment, made in a television interview, is heightened by the fact that Mr. Pompidou is running hard for the right to govern this "ungovernable" people. The French have been known for centuries for this quality of fierce independence, combined with deep mistrust of the Government, of foreigners, and of one another. It is a product, and a cause, of their long history of wars, invasions, and civil upheavals, generally coming to muddy, inconclusive endings. It accounts for some of the charm and variety of the country. (The old quip "How can you rule a country that has 300 cheeses?" is an understatement; actually, there are thousands of cheeses.) It accounts for the fact that the French are among the most unruly and dangerous motorists in the world. It may help account for the defeat of 1940, and for the relatively superior survival rate of the French under the occupation and even in concentration camps.

The process of coping with a hostile world is known, again with proud irony, as Système D, from the verb *se débrouiller*. This means to get around such entanglements as traffic laws, taxes, monetary controls, shortages, rationing. Only the French, probably, could have mounted a monetary crisis, as they did last fall, with an economy booming, $4 billion of gold in the kitty, and a strong government determined to hold the

line. Ten years of stability could not make them trust paper money, nor cause them to forget how to get around the barriers raised by bureaucrats.

Their ingrained mistrust was a factor in the defeat of General de Gaulle. On the face of it, the proposal to decentralize government power among the old provinces was popular, but many people saw this only as a plan for still another bureaucracy. A factory foreman in Orléans demanded, "Are we going to let some guy 60 miles away tell us whether we'll build a swimming pool here?" The Gaullist city of Nancy voted no because the provincial capital had been awarded to Metz. The issue on the ballot played only a minor role, however. What made a decisive portion of the petit bourgeoisie, bastion of the

regime, turn against it? Their surface complaint was about high taxes, some of which they actually pay. But interviews soon brought out their real grievance: the new supermarket down the street. Faced with shopkeeper strikes, the Government did nothing to block supermarkets, but it eased taxes. This made more difficult the problem of combating inflation and protecting the franc.

French tax laws assume that the taxpayer is a liar. Under many headings outward signs of wealth are used as a basis for computing income, in preference to the sworn returns. As a result, poormouthing is a national habit, and even the largest, richest corporations practice the systematic concealment of earnings. This has led French investors to pour money into Wall Street, in part because the French, with reason, trust American balance sheets more than their own. It has also forced the Government to raise and lend money to industry—some of which was transferred out of the country during the franc crisis last fall. Another result has been a tax system that depends 60 percent on the consumer (through sales taxes) and about 20 percent on wage earners, who cannot escape because their employers report their payrolls to the Government.

A resentful working class, a fearful peasantry and shopkeeper class, and a wily and cynical bourgeoisie would seem to add up to an ungovernable society. Yet there are those who, paradoxically (the French love paradoxes), claim that France is actually remarkably stable. They do not rest their argument on the eleven years of Gaullism. They maintain that the Third and Fourth Republics, for all their revolving-door ministries, had more continuity than met the eye; the bureaucracy never changed, and the basic alliances that formed the governments were the same.

Valéry Giscard d'Estaing has said that France had four political families: the Communists, the Socialists, the "liberals"—in the Continental sense, meaning conservatives, or advocates of laissez faire—and the Gaullists.

The "liberal" and Socialist families are each split into several parties, and there are several fringe groupings on the far Left and far Right. The schema is also flawed in that the Gaullists cannot really be made into a separate traditional family.

Most Gaullists share the economic orthodoxy of the "liberals." They departed from tradition in favoring a strong style of government under a strong leader—unless one chooses to trace this to the Bonapartist tradition. In principle, the strong presidency has now been accepted by the other "families." It has prevailed in the United States for a century and a half under the two-party system. Whether it can work in multiparty, undisciplined France—whether Gaullism can long survive without de Gaulle—remains to be seen.

LA LIBERTE FRANCAISE

Paris—April, 1972

Freedom, a man recited, is when the doorbell rings at 6 o'clock in the morning and you know it's the milkman. Certainly, we are free here, he said.

Well, a woman objected, my bell rang at 3 o'clock the other morning, and it was two policemen. They asked if my son lived there. When I asked what had happened, where he was, they said they didn't know, they just had their orders. No, she said, she did not panic, because it had happened before, as to many another mother of a student Leftist or hippie. The youth returned late in the morning and said his car had been stopped in a quarter where there had been a demonstration earlier. He and his friends were held overnight "for identification."

The foregoing conversation, at a dinner party in the conservative sixteenth Arrondissement, illustrates the complexity of any assessment of liberty in France. That this is a free country— without quotation marks—is questioned only by extremists or persons momentarily exasperated by some bit of police nastiness or bureaucratic bloodymindedness. France is in fact a shrine of Western liberalism, the birthplace of the slogan "Liberty, Equality, Fraternity," which her armies, fighting a coalition of monarchies, spread through Europe at the end of the eighteenth century.

The slogan now adorns every town hall in France. But it is seldom mentioned without ironic intent. This is because the ideas of 1789 were never permanently secured. The French today live under their Fifth Republic; their freedoms have often been crushed or gravely menaced. Roger Errera, in a recent study called *The Abandonment of Liberties*, maintains that civil war has been latent here since 1934, and as a result, civil rights have been in steady regression. Be that as it may, it is only 14 years since a mutinous army brought

145

the resignation of the discredited Fourth Republic, only ten years since the last resistance of army terrorists was broken, and less than four years since France was paralyzed by a general strike, with the army again poised to march on Paris.

This democracy, so often imperiled, is also obviously limited. When Jacques Delarue Caron de Beaumarchais was named recently to succeed Geoffroy Louis Chodron de Courcel as Ambassador to London, it drew no more attention than would the appointment to a similar post of an American industrialist less endowed with pedigree but more useful to the political party in power. A foreman living in one of the Communist suburbs that ring Paris remarked without bitterness: "It's not for nothing that a certain class of society sends its sons to Science Po'. They learn lots of things that others have to learn one by one, the hard way." The reference was to the Ecole des Sciences Politiques, one of the élite schools whose graduates predominate in government and finance. In fact, fewer than one out of ten students in the entire university system come from the working classes. The foreman had been asked whether as a Frenchman he felt free. "Only half," he replied, "since you can't go out without an identity card, or else you risk spending the night in a police station." He quickly relented. "Aside from the Government being a little too much of a police state, it's not unfree. You don't need a pass to travel to Nice, or leave the country. Can I say what I think? All the same, sure I can."

The passion of the French police for keeping track of everybody is legendary. A veteran of the French Resistance who applied for a government job ran into trouble because his biographical résumé did not correspond with false information his wife had given the police during the Occupation. A woman who sent an unused ticket back to the government railway system for a refund last month received a check in the name of her husband, which was not in her letter nor even in the telephone book. It is, incidentally, only recently that French women have been able to have checking accounts without their husbands' permission. They obtained the right to vote and hold office at the end of World War II, and nearly all inequalities specified in the law have gradually been repealed, but there is only one woman in the cabinet today, and she ranks fortieth among the forty ministers. It should be added that, at least in urban circles, French women have for centuries asserted themselves as individuals in a manner that is envied by their sisters around the world. Yet they are virtually excluded from key positions in business and the professions, and are paid far less than men for equal work.

The inquisitiveness of the police goes beyond keeping account of the whereabouts of everybody in France. It has been publicly estimated, and never officially denied, that more than 10,000 telephones are tapped by a special agency that does nothing else. The mails are not sacrosanct, either. A lawyer said his client's letters from Switzerland were systematically opened during the last monetary crisis.

"Still," the foreman objected, "you can't say the French are wretched. They live well."

Here, as he suggested, a definition of terms is needed. Every society has always given its citizens total liberty to cry "Long live the king" or its equivalent. For the conformist majority, then, liberty is only an abstraction. "It's the frontier where it's attacked that counts," said Casamayor, the country's best-known writer on the theory and practice of justice. When he dons his black robe he is Magistrate Serge Fuster. But he prefers the pen name—although it once cost him his place on the bench, when Casamayor accused the Government of rigging a political trial. He was reinstated following public protest.

In an interview, Casamayor quoted Mirabeau as saying "Liberty is obedience to the law," meaning that the law is the citizen's only defense against the tyranny of the state. "In France, we speak of justice," he said. "In England, they speak of law. Justice is a quality, like hope and charity. It's extremely unhealthy to give the name of a virtue to a public service. An immediate result is that its functionaries believe they have that virtue."

Aram Kevorkian, a prominent American lawyer here, said the French judiciary system was in some ways admirable, notably in that the 4500 judges are career civil servants, chosen by exams. "The French would be horrified," he said, "to learn that in many places in the United States one buys a judgeship." As a result, he went on, justice in French civil courts tends to be highly professional, and fair. "For example," he explained, "I've found no prejudice against American companies in litigation with French."

Many French judges are more critical, especially since 1968, when a wave of self-questioning swept the country. More than one-fourth of the judges then formed a union, whose congress last fall uttered some harsh comments about their profession. The judiciary comprises examining magistrates, the prosecuting branch (the Parquet), and trial judges. The union complained that members were graded every two years—by the Parquet! "Like pupils," Casamayor said, "and the administration promotes people who are safe." Judges confessed that they addressed plaintiffs and defendants according to their social position: "Monsieur" for a person of status, the family name for a workman, and the familiar "thee" for an Arab or other member of the lower orders.

This touched the nerve of the question—that majestic equality in law that, in the famous jibe, forbids the rich as well as the poor to sleep under the bridges and beg in the streets for their bread. Michel Rocard, an independent Leftist deputy, recently asked Justice Minister René Pleven in a written question why a $10 theft would bring the culprit into criminal court, while a major tax fraud or pollution case would be settled by negotiation, in secrecy. So far, the minister has not replied. The presumption of guilt is inherent in the French system, to the extent that a lawyer quoted an examining magistrate as cutting off his client with the words, "You say you are innocent —well, prove it!"

Under the French procedure the accused, once indicted, has the right to counsel and access to the evidence at all stages of investigation, until the case, practically completed, goes to the trial, which is mercifully short. There is no Fifth Amendment; a refusal to testify counts heavily against a defendant. And there is no right of habeas corpus. There is no limit in law on the time an accused man may be held without trial. About one-third of the French prison population of 30,000 or so is in that situation. Waits of six months to a year are not uncommon, and Casamayor has denounced one that took four years. According to lawyers, the delay is not due to crowded calendars alone, but to the desire of the accusers for time to wring out a confession. Frequently, they report, the sentence is neatly tailored to the time already served.

The presumption of innocence has never penetrated the French press. Even the best newspapers headline "Child's Murderer Arrested" or "Heartless Mother Jailed" on the strength of a policeman's word. Libel convictions are obtainable on less evidence than would satisfy an American court, but damages are negligible. Dr. Pierre Vidal-Naquet, historian and longtime campaigner for civil liberties, recently won a suit against a newspaper that had accused him of fabricating evidence on the torture of Algerians by the French army. It took him ten years. He collected the symbolic one franc.

A French law does give persons criticized in the press the right to reply—in the same newspaper.

147

This does not, however, apply to radio and television, which are owned by the state and have been politically controlled by the governing party from the beginning. This was not serious before the war, Dr. Vidal-Naquet said in an interview, because broadcasting was a relatively feeble medium then and there were many more newspapers. Today, there are no more than three or four financially sound dailies in Paris, and fewer than a dozen regional papers dominate the provinces. More and more, these papers have become nonpartisan and innocuous. In any case, there has never been a muckraking tradition in France. Some revolutionary periodicals have been seized, and their publishers, including Jean-Paul Sartre, prosecuted. A book by the Brazilian Carlos Marighela, *Pour la Libération du Brésil*, was seized as offensive to a foreign government, but 20 leading Parisian publishers jointly put out another edition, and it was let alone.

"Naturally," said Jean Lindon of Editions de Minuit, "we protest against censorship, but we are certainly among the most privileged publishers in the world."

One reason is that costs seem to be lower than in Britain and the United States, so that small editions can be produced economically—although serious writers have to hold other jobs, in teaching and journalism, to make ends meet. The theater, also, still gets by, although it does not thrive, on audiences that would not sustain a show in New York or London. More serious, Mr. Lindon said, is the problem of self-censorship—the book that is not published because it might offend or, especially, the movie that is not made because the official subsidy is withheld or credit is denied in fear that the film will be banned. The Italian-made film *The Battle of Algiers* was denied a permit for years and then kept out of most theaters under the threat—several times carried out—of violence by Rightists. The brilliant television documentary *Le Chagrin et la Pitié* was barred from the French networks because it upset the prevailing mythology about the Occupation.

A sculptor said, "Freedom? In France? It's total! Unfortunately! It's like punching in a void. An artist always needs to react against something."

France is, then, one of the freest countries in the world—her people being rather more inclined, in the opinion of Roger Errera, to submit to the authority of the state than the British or the Americans, but less than the Germans.

Constitutional authorities decry the lack of checks and balances. As in Britain, the judiciary has never claimed the right to overrule the Government. Under the Fifth Republic, the Legislature has allowed itself to become little more than a rubber stamp. Yet in some respects the French system is more democratic than the American and British ones. The multiplicity of parties, for example, gives a citizen a better chance to vote for a candidate close to his own views. And while the true cost of politicking is going up sharply, it is nothing like the American scene. Campaigns are brief, official billboards are put up in each district, and a modest subsidy is paid to each substantial candidate for printing costs. Further, free broadcast time is fairly allotted during the campaign. This does not, however, prevent the ruling party from hogging the airwaves at other times, and from guiding the news shamelessly—which sparked a revolt in 1968 that has at any rate inhibited the propaganda somewhat.

The April (1972) referendum on British entry into the Common Market was a special case. Observers noted the irony that the French, who favored British entry overwhelmingly, were allowed to vote on it, while the British, who are deeply divided on the issue, were not.

The "frontier where liberty is attacked," in Casamayor's words, is not, then, so much in the main political battlefield, but in those guerrilla zones patrolled by the police. Aside from common crime, which is a relatively minor problem in France, the areas most troubled are those of restless youth and immigrant labor, especially the North Africans. The French police have been at war with the Algerians since about 1954, and with troublesome youth since 1968. The word war is not too strong, except that by unwritten law the police do not kill French youths.

Unlike the American experience in Vietnam, the French Government was able to bury all of its atrocities in Algeria during the war, by seizing publications that exposed them. By now, however, a substantial documentation has accumulated, and it is no longer possible to deny that torture and murder on a massive scale were practiced by the army and police during that period, both in Algeria and on the Continent. In fact, a book affirming and defending the use of torture in that war was published last winter by General Jacques Massu, recently retired hero of the Battle of Algiers. With the help of four television appearances by the General, it was a smash best seller.

The war has left a deep residue of hatred for Arabs in France. They form a major part of the three million immigrant laborers who "Do the dirty jobs the French won't handle," but, in fact, help keep French pay scales lower than anywhere else in the Common Market except Italy. The immigrant is most often jammed into shantytowns and slums, preyed upon by racketeers and hiring agents, and subject to arbitrary expulsion. Too poor, generally, to bring his wife and family, he is regarded with fear and hostility by his proper French neighbors.

"As long as they're invisible, they're left alone," the foreman said. "But whenever something happens, as when a taxi driver was attacked in our town, the cops raid the Algerian shelter."

Vignette on a boulevard near the Opéra the other day: A dozen Parisians cross the street against the light, ignoring the whistle of a policeman. He runs after them and stops one of them, the only Arab-looking man in the crowd. "Where are thy papers? . . ."

Long hair or a picket sign is nearly as provocative to the police. Before my office window the other day, a group of youths trying to crash a rock 'n roll show were knocked down, beaten, and kicked about the head by riot policemen. A *Times* reporter and scores of others accompanying President Pompidou in the Lorraine last month saw orderly youths who had been holding up banners in the crowd savagely beaten, first on the scene and then in the police station.

Liberty, then, as any Frenchman would say, is relative.

149

SHADOW OVER CLAIRVAUX

Only the barking of dogs broke the silence of the wooded valley, tinted with the first gold of autumn. In the bar across the road from the prison, men moodily drank their beer or red wine and glared suspiciously at a stranger. The air was filled with hatred, fear, and secrecy.

The hatred and fear are no mystery. A few days ago two long-term convicts appeared in the infirmary of the Maison Centrale de Clairvaux and took the guard and nurse prisoner at knifepoint. By telephone they tried to trade the lives of their hostages for getaway cars and guns. The weapons were refused. When the police smashed their way in Tuesday morning, the guard was dead and the nurse dying, their throats slashed.

This is virtually all of the story that the public has been given to know. Newspapers have reported also that the nation's prison guards stopped work to protest the liberalization of penal conditions, that some hooted at government ministers attending the mass funerals of the victims, and that President Pompidou criticized reforms and defended capital punishment at his news conference.

But behind the gray walls of the medieval monastery of Clairvaux, transformed into a prison compound, and in the few score of houses outside where the rest of the staff lives, other facts that may have a bearing on the tragedy have been carefully bottled up. In the bar, a husky, mustached young guard said his wife, a nurse, would have been on duty in the infirmary that morning had she not been on maternity leave.

"They're like wild animals," somebody said.

"No," he retorted, "they're worse. Animals don't kill their own kind. We should take 50 of them out into the court and set them against the wall, and 50 guards, one to a prisoner, and (he brought a hand down in a definitive gesture) make an example of them."

In a nearby community, another staff member admitted, reluctantly and anonymously, that exemplary treatment in this spirit had been tried before at Clairvaux. Until now, the affair has been kept secret. Last May, five prisoners were caught trying to escape through a sewer conduit. They were savagely beaten in the courtyard before the other prisoners, to teach them a lesson. The beating, obviously a crime in itself, caused a dispute within the prison administration. It conceivably was an element in the subsequent liberalization of conditions.

"It's a rest home now," a guard complained.

"It's a luxury hotel," said a young workman from a neighboring village. "Hot water, radio, television, newspapers . . ."

The hot water was an exaggeration, but the other items had been granted, for the first time. Much progress has also been made in transferring prisoners from the "chicken cages"—barred cells —as more comfortable dormitories and rooms are built. The easing of conditions admittedly heightened the security problem, which was aggravated by the indiscriminate crowding of longtermers with other prisoners. The number of guards was not increased. When the tragedy struck, their fear and anger were directed at the liberalization. Since the jailbreak attempt with its bloody ending the remaining 500 prisoners have been kept locked up, denied work, visitors, newspapers, radio, and television. The gendarmes have taken over security details and the guards are reporting only for minimum maintenance.

"We'll strike until they get all five," a guard said, referring to a total of five convicts now awaiting trial for murdering prison guards in France. A staff member who described himself as a reformer and normally an opponent of capital punishment said that in some of those cases he could find attenuating circumstances, such as the "provocation" of certain sadistic guards.

"But this guard was known as a nice guy," he said, "and the nurse! They killed in cold blood. I'm afraid that those two heads must fall."

It was suggested that the two desperados might have been influenced by the public beatings administered to the prisoners who tried to escape last May, and that in any case it was tragic that men with a record of savage violence had been able to make their way unguarded—in a manner not yet made public—to the infirmary.

"Just because there was a failure in security," the staff member replied, "didn't give them the right to kill."

"We'll strike," said the man in the bar, "until the public realizes what kind of beasts we're dealing with."

When the visitor objected that there wasn't much sympathy around the country for the convicts, he retorted angrily, "Oh, yes. There was a woman came by yesterday, and do you know what she called them? 'Poor wretches'!"

[Because witnesses declined to be quoted, the foregoing dispatch had to be phrased with circumspection. Not mentioned, for example, is the savagery inflicted on the earlier group of escapees, some of them beaten nearly to death with pick-handles. The indication that deliberate negligence by guards may have played a role in the infirmary murders was pretty strong.

In the end, despite evidence that one of the convicts was a psychopath and the other was his stupid and frightened tool, both men went to the guillotine. Following a wave of prison uprisings, however, a number of reforms were adopted.]

151

BARRICADES IN THE LATIN QUARTER

Paris—May, 1968

The Latin Quarter today was a battlefield, with tourists. Tens of thousands of them filtered past the grim blue ranks of riot police, clicking cameras at the debris of a night of street fighting. The damp air stung the eyes with the lingering smoke of burnt rubber mingled with the fresher fumes of thousands of cars, slowly working their way around the sealed-off Sorbonne. The hundreds of stolid policemen ignored the street jams; traffic was not their concern.

The Boulevard St. Michel was a mud road in the area of the Place Edmond Rostand beside the Luxembourg Garden. Its paving blocks were now heaped alongside, and the traces of barricades were visible at each of the six corners around the Place. Rue Monsieur le Prince was still blocked. Huge concrete stanchions, benches, and tree guards were strewn about the six-point crossing, but the barricade builders left untouched the bronze statues decorating the fountain in the middle.

Place Edmond Rostand was only a skirmish line for the main battle zone, which ran the 7-yard length of the Rue Gay Lussac, a broad, straight street that begins at the Gare Luxembourg. Bulldozers and street gangs were hard at work, but the street this afternoon was still lined with burnt cars and other debris. Each of the narrow side streets entering it had its own contingent of wrecks and barricades. Here and there, store windows were cracked, but there was no sign of looting. The steel shutters of one store bore, in fresh red paint, "Vive la Révolution."

Clumps of onlookers watched the workmen and talked animatedly about the night's events. In one group, a workman was saying, "Maybe some of them are *fils de papa*, but you have to take your hat off to them. They showed real courage." Fils de papa is slang for the son of a well-to-do family, with the implication of playboy. When the student troubles were still minor, Communists here dismissed them as the carryings on of idle bourgeois youth. Extremist students who barged into the May Day parade, for example, were repelled with the chant, "Fils de papa, go to work!"

A woman asked passersby if they had seen any official who would register her claim for her car, which had been destroyed. In principle, she explained, the Government will pay for riot damages, but she was unable to find a policeman to take formal note of her loss. There were thousands around, but they were all "too busy," she complained. Actually, they were all standing at key crossings, in triple rows, with carbines slung, or they were resting in huge vans covered with mesh. Some units carried short rubber truncheons, others three-foot batons. Helmets and goggles were de rigueur; one company wore new face grills like catchers' masks. All units had sacks of grenades at hand. An officer told a newsman that the sector was all quiet, but added with a smile, "It will begin again."

REVOLUTIONARY KERMESSE

A revolutionary kermesse has taken over the factories of this town in Normandy. Effigies hang from flag poles, crude signs decorate the fences, and clumps of cheerful workers, mostly young, guard the gates. In the flush of power, the workers of Elbeuf have found it possible to be magnanimous. Until this writing the supervisors at the Renault plant had not been allowed even to go to the toilet except under guard. But now after a two-hour debate, the workers heeded an appeal by union officials to let the supervisors go home.

The movement here began when the management of the state-owned Renault plant refused to negotiate new union demands. Fired by the example of Sud-Aviation workers at St. Nazare, the employees decided spontaneously to occupy the plant. Delegations went to the nearby Cipel battery factory, which followed suit, except that their supervisors were allowed to go home in shifts, like the workers. The movement spread day by day to Kleber (plastics) and Rhône Poulenc (drugs and chemicals). Textile and metal plants never organized before joined up and even the railroad depot closed down.

At the dingy headquarters of the Communist-led labor federation, volunteers were counting new membership cards. "The remarkable thing," said one, "is that the average age is less than 19."

"The remarkable thing," reported a Renault machine operator named Gilbert, "is the women. I never thought I would see women go on strike quicker than the men."

At several factory gates, the workers were asked what had set them off. None mentioned the students of Paris. When a reporter did mention the students, he got the typical answer: "They've nothing to do with us. They're mostly sons of the rich." A union officer conceded, "The workers may have said to themselves, 'Well, we're not going to let the students show us the way.'"

The demands of the two groups were different, it was pointed out. The students want a reorganized educational system, the workers higher wages, shorter hours, and union recognition. But like the students, the workers have been meeting around the clock and their demands are broadening. Over the sprawling Renault plant, a banner proclaims: "The Left to Power!"

"De Gaulle did some good things," said an elderly worker, "but nothing for the workers."

Gilbert, who is the father of two children, said that when he started at Renault seven years ago, he earned $140 a month for a 48-hour week. Today he earns $160. The Renault workers are among the best paid here. A majority of Elbeuf workers, a union spokesman said, earn less than $120 a month and work upwards of 50 hours a week.

Only the oldest workers could recall a movement of comparable breadth—the strikes of the mid-thirties. Since then, there have been occasional stoppages and occasional pay rises, but no collective bargaining such as is known in the U.S., virtually no union contracts, and no closed shops. Workers are divided among the Communist-led C.G.T. and the Catholic-led C.F.D.T. But most of them have not paid any dues at all. At Rhône-Poulenc, a worker said: "We had to collect dues under the table."

15:3

They were clearly determined to stay in the factories until their demands were met: $200 a month minimum wage, a 40-hour week with 48 hours' pay, and retirement at 60. When it was suggested that Rhône-Poulenc's German competitors would then be able to sell cheaper, a worker replied, "The management has already said that." "The Common Market," said another worker, "brings misery." Nevertheless, the workers were concerned about their immediate future. Each department in the chemical plant finished its run to avoid damage to the chemicals being processed. At Renault, blue camp tents were being raised for the guards. But the grounds were otherwise immaculate. Strike committees had ordered a big clean-up of machinery. Other committees were organizing sports and entertainment; a movie was coming in at night. In the smaller plants men were bowling and women were knitting. It was a holiday, but a woman said: "We'll stay until we win."

WORRIED COPS

Paris—May, 1968

Spokesmen for the police told the Government that there was a limit to their obedience. In an extraordinary declaration, the major police unions expressed sympathy with the national strike movement and prayed that the Government "would not systematically oppose the police to workers fighting for their demands. Otherwise," they went on, "policemen would have the right to consider the execution of certain missions as grave issues of conscience. They could not in any case serve any regime that did not respect democratic republican institutions."

The statement was not taken here as a threat of a police strike, nor has there been any indication of disaffection among the forces of order. In fact, since the recent troubles there has been no fraternizing between the police and private citizens here, who seem to ignore each other's existence. Crime reporters, whose daily work keeps them in close contact with the police, said the declaration reflected two chief motives: a demand to share in the wage increases resulting from the strike wave, and a desire to reduce the obloquy that has rained upon the police from all sides as a result of the battles in the Latin Quarter.

The police are not wildly popular in any country, but in France they confront a hostility to authority that amounts to a proud national trait. One of George Brassen's ballads, about a free-for-all at a village fair, says "everybody gets together when it comes to slugging the cops."

THE "EX" BEAUX ARTS

Paris—June, 1968

Today was Whitmonday, most of France was on holiday and the politicians were planning post-strike election campaigns. But in the "ex-Ecole des Beaux Arts," the revolutionary flame was still burning bright and clear. The ex-Beaux-Arts, facing the Louvre across the Seine, is now a teeming commune of artists and students, creating, around the clock, wall posters that call upon France to continue the struggle that rocked the regime. The revolution came late to the Beaux Arts. That it came at all was a subject of wonderment here. For the Beaux Arts is—or was? —one of the "grandes écoles," those élite colleges attended, in general, by the brighter sons and daughters of the well-to-do. The Beaux Arts élèves have traditionally kicked up many a rumpus, but they were the kind of capers that bring reminiscent smiles to the lips of their elders, like the recent underground and illegal Beaux Arts ball. Stealing into the Catacombs, they cavorted amid the bones of their ancestors to the music of the popular and atrocious Beaux Arts brass band.

155

By common consent, politics was banned at the Beaux Arts. The massiers, a variety of student monitors, would severely reprove any serious partisan talk. So it was only in mid-May, after the week of the barricades in the nearby Latin Quarter, that the élèves sat down to consider the situation.

"We suddenly realized that everything was false," said Alain, a bearded young painter. "Little by little, we took possession. Then, we asked the professors to leave, because we found they wanted to recover control. What did we want? Most of all, a change of society. . . . A school without bosses . . . self-management, and no professors. Well, that is the opinion of most of the students. The professors could come and look, even preside, but they mustn't say, 'Paint like this,' or 'Paint like that.' "

The architecture students revolted against the system of "patrons" or bosses, wherein each élève is apprenticed to a leading architect. The movement enlisted many young graduates, who in a stormy meeting dissolved the national Order of Architects. Membership in the order is compulsory for the practice of architecture here. A similar upheaval in the medical profession resulted in the occupation of its headquarters, equivalent to that of the American Medical Association. The old officers, aided by plainclothes policemen, finally threw the rebels out. As for the arts students, they discovered a special function in the revolution. "We found that all the media of information were in the hands of the Establishment," Alain said. "The only means at hand for us to reach the people were posters. So we set up a little lithograph shop and a little silkscreen shop."

The results are now visible all over Paris. A few hours after General de Gaulle's remark, "Reform, yes; bedsoiling, no!" the city was plastered with caricatures of the general bearing the legend, "The Bed-soiler Is He." In the subway system, idle for two weeks, underground crews have pasted a variety of posters over the old commercial ones. In many places, students have painted over the familiar sign "Défense d'Afficher" (forbidden to post) and made it read "Défense d'Interdire" (forbidden to prohibit). A number of the posters have become collectors' items, notably several with striking caricatures of the police, General de Gaulle, and Daniel Cohn-Bendit, the student anarchist expelled from France; the last one bears the caption, "We Are All Undesirables."

Gallery owners approached the Beaux Arts leaders with an offer to buy their output en masse, for resale in the American market. The students refused, and instructed their "service d'ordre," or volunteer guards, to keep strangers out and prevent the smuggling of posters for sale. Studios today were crowded with young artists making posters and puppets, for revolutionary puppet shows. Wet posters hung on clotheslines to dry. A line slanting down into one of the inner gardens was used to slide screens down, to be dried on the lawn. To avoid commercialism and personal aggrandisement, it was decreed that all posters be anonymous. In the "ex-Studio Chapelain Midi," a dozen artists were preparing entries; a few hours later, the "poster committee," including anybody who cared to attend, would discuss their work and decide which posters to publish.

While participants belong to a variety of radical groups, they share a belief that the general strike should be continued until the revolution is won. They also share a contempt for the de Gaulle regime and its parliamentary opposition— including the Communists. There was considerable discussion, Alain said, about a new poster powerfully combining the features of General de Gaulle and Hitler, with arm out in the Nazi salute. There were no words, only a question mark. Alain was asked whether some people thought it was a bit overdone.

"No," he replied, "we thought it was too soft. It was the question mark we objected to."

156

THE END OF A DREAM

The National Assembly broke up in a scene that symbolized the schism of the French people: Left and Right, face to face across an empty arena, defiantly singing the "Marseillaise" at each other. The business of the final session lasted less than two minutes, and the only words of any importance in its minutes were by General de Gaulle. The script had in fact been announced by the General during his radio address an hour earlier: "Today I dissolve the National Assembly."

The deputies listened to the speech in small groups crowded around transistor radios, in the ornate marble halls, writing rooms, caucus rooms, and lobbies of the old Palais Bourbon. There were occasional exclamations, and even laughter at one point, the reference to "the ambition and hatred of castoff politicians." But generally there was only a tense silence. When it was over, an angry man cried, "It's civil war!"

Guy Mollet, the Socialist leader, agreed, but with a faint smile and a shrug, "This will end in civil war." An opposition conservative, a Bordeaux winegrower, managed to be hopeful, and paradoxical. "The tone of the speech threatens to create a climate of disorder and eventually insurrection," he said, "but given the choice between anarchy and absolute monarchy, the French will choose legal democracy."

Dire rumors flew through the halls. "Did you hear about the tanks at Camp des Loges?" a man asked. A woman swore that she had heard at only second hand of a Gaullist deputy boasting, "I've got a thousand guys in the Vendée who've been champing at the bit for two weeks. Now we'll let them go." Told that this would mean bloodshed,

the Gaullist was supposed to have replied, "I don't give a damn. There will be less than under a Communist dictatorship."

The ceremonial detachment of Republican guards marched into the lobby to salute the arrival of the speaker, Jacques Chaban-Delmas. Bells rang, summoning the deputies. The Gaullists arrived first, many wearing or carrying tricolor sashes. For a minute, it seemed as if the Left was carrying out its plan to boycott the session. But then, its deputies filed in. The lights went out, as they had several times during the day, then went

on again. Breaking a deep silence, Mr. Chaban-Delmas thanked the deputies for their past cooperation, and said, "I have received the following letter:

'I have the honor to advise you that by virtue of Article 12 of the Constitution and after having proceeded with the consultations foreseen by that article, I have pronounced the dissolution of the assembly.

Charles de Gaulle.' "

Strong applause, and shouts of "Vive la République!" arose from the majority. The opposition was silent.

"The session is adjourned," Mr. Chaban-Delmas said.

The Gaullist deputies and conservatives began crowding out. But the left-wing deputies remained silently seated. A departing deputy faced them and cried, "We'll meet you at the elections!"

At this point François Mitterand, head of the Federation of the Democratic and Socialist Left, cried, "Vive la République!" Socialists and Communists rose together, echoed the chant, and began singing the "Marseillaise." The Gaullists turned and faced them across the empty seats and took up the anthem. It was strong, but not fraternal; each side appeared to accuse the other of raising "the bloody standard of tyranny" over France and both appeared to call the citizens to arms. When it was over, the majority gathered in the courtyard and marched behind a tricolor flag to the Gaullist demonstration in the Place de la Concorde.

[A million members of the hitherto silent majority marched up the Champs-Elysees, and the May revolution was over. Yet aside from winning major gains for workers and major reforms for the educational system, it all but shattered the Fifth Republic. In the end, it brought Charles de Gaulle down. He did not long survive.]

THE FUNERAL OF A HERO

Colombey-les-Deux-Eglises—November, 1970

Charles de Gaulle was buried as he wished, in simplicity, surrounded by his family, his fellow villagers, his comrades of the Liberation, and thousands of his grieving countrymen.

While presidents and kings paid him homage far away in Paris, he was quietly interred beside his daughter Anne in the tiny churchyard of this humble farm village, lost in the rolling green pastures and gold-tinged forests of eastern France. As he directed, there were "neither President, nor ministers, nor Assembly committees, nor public authorities." There was no speech, no sermon, no music other than the hymns and responses of the village choir, accompanied by a small harmonium. The mass lasted barely an hour.

158

By dawn hundreds of pilgrims in their Sunday attire were streaming up the hill past the church for a glimpse of the stone wall and trees that guard La Boisserie, the de Gaulle home. By early afternoon tens of thousands had arrived by car, train, and bus. They were of all ages and came from all parts of France. Many of the older ones wore medals and ribbons; among them were a bus load of Algerian veterans of World War II.

It had been a brilliant fall day, but then clouds appeared and a chilly breeze whipped the flags in the square before the little Church of Notre Dame. Lining it were 200 men representing the army, the navy, the air force, and St. Cyr, the military academy whose most illustrious cadet was de Gaulle. As the bells tolled briefly, the Reverend François de Gaulle, a nephew, presided, in the intimacy of the family at La Boisserie, over the rite of raising the body.

The gates opened at 2:50 P.M. and a squat, crablike armored-reconnaissance vehicle rolled slowly down the leaf-carpeted driveway. Its right fender bore the number 13. The turret had been removed and the white oak coffin was in its place, covered with the tricolor. The six-wheeled vehicle turned left down the Rue du Général de Gaulle, a country road lined with stone farmhouses and barns, from which a cock's crow and the stamp of cattle could occasionally be heard. As the vehicle appeared men bared their heads. Some extended arms in a V-for-victory salute. In silence, they watched the coffin pass, followed by four cars carrying Mrs. de Gaulle and the family.

The 400 yards to the church were traversed in seven minutes. Inside, waiting in their customary pews, were most of the 300 parishioners of Colombey, the Municipal Council in front. In the side aisles were crowded the Companions of the Order of Liberation, designated by de Gaulle as the principal combatants in his struggle of 1940–1945. Many, such as André Malraux, had achieved other distinctions, but they were there only as honored members of the Resistance. Some could not find room inside and waited in the square with the multitude.

Ten village youths bore the coffin on their shoulders through the portal to the varnished wood altar, where three tall candles stood. Three more were set on each side. Before the main altar were bows of sycamore with gold and russet leaves. The family took its places in the front left pews and the Most Reverend Alfred Joseph Atton, Bishop of Langres, began the mass, assisted by Father de Gaulle and the village curate, the Reverend Claude Jaugey, in purple robes. It was, as the curate had promised, a conventional service in the new French liturgy, virtually the same as any funeral mass for any parishioner. In prayer the celebrant said only: "We pray for Charles de Gaulle, your servant whom you have called."

Father Jaugey had, with some uneasiness, ordered a sound system installed to convey the proceedings to the thousands outside. "I think General de Gaulle would have wished it," he said.

The crowd listened in patient silence, although the crush was such that people who fainted had to be passed from hand to hand overhead in stretchers to first-aid squads in cleared zones.

In place of a sermon the Bishop asked a moment of silence.

At the end the mourners joined in the Lord's Prayer and were invited to receive Communion. Mrs. de Gaulle and her family led a file to the altar. When the last communicant had returned to his place, the young pall-bearers took up the coffin and carried it down the aisle. They were followed only by the family and the servants from La Boisserie. Mrs. de Gaulle, a dignified figure in black with a heavy veil, walked unaided beside her son, Philippe, in his naval captain's uniform. With them were de Gaulle's sister, Mrs. Marie-Agnes Cailliau, the de Gaulles' daughter, Mrs. Elizabeth de Boissieu and her husband, and Philippe's wife and their children.

The cortège turned beyond the church to enter the little graveyard. At the far corner was the five-foot-tall white marble cross marking the grave where Anne de Gaulle was buried in 1948 at the age of 20. Bishop Atton said a brief final prayer as the coffin was lowered into the sunken vault. He, Mrs. de Gaulle, and the others in turn sprinkled holy water on it. Then a white marble slab was rolled into place beside that on Anne de Gaulle's grave. As de Gaulle had ordered, it carried only the legend:

"Charles de Gaulle 1890–1970."

A bouquet of white chrysanthemums stood by the grave, one of several placed there by anonymous hands, when de Gaulle's death became known. Many more stately wreaths had arrived—eight of them, at 2 o'clock this morning, from Mao Tse-tung and other Chinese leaders. All were placed in that part of the little graveyard on the other side of the church.

As the cortège returned to La Boisserie, other mourners began to file past the grave. Among them was the Reverend Raymond-Leopold Bruckberger, the Dominican priest who received de Gaulle in Paris in 1944 as chaplain of the Resistance. Father Bruckberger, in a white robe with the red ribbon of the Order of the Liberation, emerged from the church with reddened eyes.

"You know that Anne was a girl 'not like the others,' " he recalled to a friend. "She was mentally retarded. And when she was buried here, de Gaulle told his wife, 'Now she is like the others.' Well now de Gaulle is like the others."

The thousands now were slowly filing past. In the jammed square and streets, few could move; there were sudden crushes, and scores fainted. But still they came, few in tears but all solemn. The sky cleared, the sun set and a harvest moon rose in the east. The forests where de Gaulle often walked darkened and disappeared.

Someone recalled what de Gaulle had written of those woods in his memoirs: "Their dark depth fills me with nostalgia; but suddenly, a bird's song, the sunshine on the foliage, the buddings of a shrub, remind me that life, since it appeared on earth, had waged a combat it has never lost. Then I am filled with a secret comfort, because everything is always beginning again. What I did will sooner or later be a source of new ardors after I am gone."

THE CHARACTER OF CHARLES DE GAULLE

Paris—October, 1971

In death as before, Charles of Lorraine continues to fascinate and trouble the French. It is doubtless far too soon to view the de Gaulle phenomenon in full historic perspective, but the urge to do so has inspired a new stream of memoirs and essays, at least two of which are remarkable works of literature.

One is André Malraux's brooding account of his last visit with de Gaulle, a Wagnerian dialogue of two gods on the ruins of Western civilization. With that superb conceit common to both of them, Malraux remarks in his preface, "We know of no dialogue of a man of history with a great artist." He implies that this lack is now remedied, and indeed it is. But the scholar is fairly warned: "This book is an interview as *Man's Fate* was a reportage."

Les Chênes Qu'on Abat (from a Victor Hugo poem: "Oh! What an awful sound they make in the dusk,/The oaks being felled for Hercules's pyre!") is part of Malraux's continuing *Antimémoires* and shares its surrealistic, murky style. It is not very different from Malraux's typical conversation, which Claude Mauriac described in his diary nineteen years ago, "going like hell, with unexpected turnoffs, obscure ellipses, hardly decipherable anecdotes, barely indicated allusions to men whose names I don't even know and whose works I ignore." But Mauriac salvaged some flashes of fascinating insights.

So it is with *Les Chênes*. Readers of the book, a smash best seller, complain that it is sometimes hard to tell which of the protagonists is supposed to be speaking. One of de Gaulle's closest collaborators opined to me that it was 90 percent Malraux; he could not accept, for example, that the General, whose serenity in the face of danger was legendary, might have shared for an evening the writer's lifelong preoccupation with death.

The old Gaullist did not question, however, that quotation of de Gaulle in *Les Chênes* which made the greatest impact: "When I left, age may have played its role. It's possible. But you understand, I had a contract with France. Things could go well or badly, she was with me. . . . When the French believe in France, ah, then! But when they stop believing. . . . The contract was broken. So it's no use any more."

Malraux tantalizes us with a riddle. He asks de Gaulle when the contract was broken: in the student-labor upheaval of May 1968 or in the Presidential election of 1965, when de Gaulle failed to get a majority in the first round? "Long before," he replies. "That's why I took Pompidou." Leaving us in mid-air Malraux muses, "Why does he say France and not the French?" and lets de Gaulle answer the unspoken question: "The French have no more national ambition. They don't want to do anything more for France. I entertained them with flags, I made them take patience, waiting for what, if not France?"

The distinction between La France and Les Français is explicit in the opening lines of de Gaulle's classic *Mémoires de Guerre* (whose Caesarian account of the triumph of a hero is resumed with dimmed splendor in *Mémoires d'Espoir* interrupted by his death): "All my life, I have conceived of France in a certain way . . . like the princess of the fairy tales or the madonna of the frescoes, as if meant for an eminent and exceptional destiny. . . . If it happens that nonetheless mediocrity marks her deeds and gestures, I suffer the sensation of an absurd anomaly, imputable to the faults of the French, not to the *génie de la patrie*."

How far the French were, during the Occupation, from the princess of the fairy tales and the madonna of the frescoes is visible with shattering impact these days in a brilliant documentary that has been playing to full and silent houses. The four and one-half hour film *Le Chagrin et la Pitié* was made by the young video journalists Max Orphuls and André Harris as a two-part television reportage. It has been broadcast elsewhere in Europe but rejected by the French O.R.T.F. state network on the ground, according to the newspaper *La Croix*, that "certain

161

myths are necessary for the happiness and tranquility of a people." (The O.R.T.F. also passed up the centennial this spring of the Paris Commune, which also pitted a resistance against a government of collaboration.)

The film makes the point beyond refutation: the conduct of the French, taken as a whole, was less than inspiring during the Occupation. The diplomat Jean Chauvel, who served in Vichy after the debacle of 1940, says in a newly published memoir *Commentaire*, that if Hitler had not distrusted France so much he could have enlisted her at that moment "as an active element in the Continental war effort." The people were psychologically prepared for it, he holds. De Gaulle himself ("France has lost a battle, she has not lost a war!") turns out to have had few illusions. In this year's second major new contribution to Gaulliana, the diary of Claude Mauriac, *Un Autre de Gaulle: Journal 1944–1954*, we learn that on July 3, 1946, he told his secretary that Churchill was right in refusing to forgive the French for having, almost unanimously, abandoned Britain in 1940. "It's a fact, though I've often proclaimed the contrary," he said with a pale smile.

France (as *Le Chagrin* observes) was the only country in occupied Europe whose legitimate (and popular) government collaborated with the enemy, whose police rounded up Jews for the death chambers and resistants for the prison camps, whose army fired on the Allies and let the panzers pass. She had resistants, brave and splendid as any, but they were fewer in the first two or three years than the number of volunteer collaborators. The overwhelming majority of the French were neither. What did they do during the war? They survived. Like Georges Pompidou, whom a journalist once described as having been a "patriote bien sage."

In an essay in *Le Monde*, the leftist intellectual Claude Bourdet remarked not long ago that French resistants were among those least susceptible to the Gaullist mystique. The typical Frenchman was bound to de Gaulle, he suggested, by a syllogism: de Gaulle was France; de Gaulle resisted; hence France resisted. Contrariwise, the military caste and those other sectors of the élite that collaborated have never forgiven de Gaulle. He poses for them the unbearable question: If de Gaulle was, in Malraux's words, "The man who in the terrible sleep of our country upheld her honor like an invincible dream" then what were they? For his part, de Gaulle deeply mistrusted the internal resistance. He did not call on the French to fight the enemy in the homeland; they were summoned to join the colors overseas and fight their way back, in a proper, uniformed army. The shot in the Métro, the shiv in the alley, the ambush in the maquis, these went against the grain of this exemplary son of St. Cyr.

The conflict in de Gaulle's attitude did not escape either his secretary Mauriac, the Catholic intellectual, or Malraux, the revolutionary writer-adventurer. Mauriac reports that, going over his mail one day just after the liberation, the General commented: "My classmates are showing up. They're all here. But when I was in London they didn't write me!" Mauriac does not record how he disposed of their appeals for clemency, but the record shows that he nearly always found grounds, if not to rehabilitate them, at least to forgive them—even Pétain.

When Malraux came to his anteroom a year later, he looked around and jested to Mauriac: "How many generals!" Another day, an admirer sent de Gaulle as a gift a proclamation of the Paris Commune; he read the names of the signers and told Mauriac ironically, "Tous les F.F.I., quoi!" The diary entry has poignancy because Mauriac was wearing an F.F.I. (French Forces of the Interior) brassard, fresh from the battle of the liberation in the Latin Quarter, when he was drafted for what was to be a 10-year hitch

162

as the General's secretary for private correspondence.

As a result of this service, we are indebted to Mauriac for an art form that one had thought to be dead: the journal of a man of letters present on the scene of history. He is a splendid witness, and it is curious to see how his straight prose report confirms Malraux's expressionist account in every way. He is splendid also because he suffers: "Mardi, 5 Septembre, 1944. Many arrests. The purity of the last days is already soiled. All this was foreseeable . . . even necessary. But I suppose my function bars me from disavowing certain excesses. I should never have accepted this job." Later, he is disturbed by the picture of a captured traitor amid an exultant crowd: "However great his crimes, as soon as he is thus prisoner of his enemies, a man is somehow washed clean of his sins."

De Gaulle then was waging the final battles of his war on three fronts. One was against the Allies, and particularly Roosevelt, to win France a seat as an equal at the peace table. Washington had opposed de Gaulle successively with Pétain, Weygand, Darlan, Giraud, and, finally, the stillborn AMGOT, an American military occupation government. All had failed. But it was only in October, 1944, that we finally recognized de Gaulle's provisional régime.

Mauriac gives us glimpses of the struggle: a letter from F.D.R., incredibly asking de Gaulle to take Giraud into his post-liberation Government; an unexplained outburst by de Gaulle, perhaps over Yalta, "Hah! the Allies are betraying Europe, the *salauds*, but they will pay me for it!"; Churchill's rejection of de Gaulle's proposal for a European federation, built around Britain and France. ("All our misunderstanding came from that," de Gaulle said. "He replied to me, 'If I must choose between Roosevelt and you, I'll never hesitate to choose Roosevelt.' . . . But he thereby lost the independence of his country.")

Excluded from Yalta, de Gaulle nevertheless won a voice for France at the peace table, and a zone of occupation in Germany. Unfortunately for the world, perhaps, he also outmaneuvered F.D.R. to reassert French authority in Indochina. . . . At the same time, de Gaulle was fighting on two other fronts, to avert a Communist takeover and to prevent a return to the parliamentary régime of party politicians which he blamed for France's humiliation. He won the first handily, although at one point he felt obliged to ask Eisenhower to release two of his French regular divisions from the front, to balance the Communist-led partisans then virtually controlling much of France.

In each showdown, de Gaulle's will proved stronger than theirs. On one such occasion to Mauriac, the General's face lit up, "You don't make a revolution without revolutionaries. And there's only one revolutionary in France: that's me." Mauriac, the Christian humanist, did not fully share the General's glee. He was so far from being a party sympathizer that he had disapproved of his father's joining the national Resistance front with the Communists during the war. (François Mauriac was in fact the only active resistant in the Académie Français.) But Claude would tell his diary, "Very often I feel closer to the Communists than to the R.P.F.s [the first Gaullist party], and I must think of the Russian concentration camps, of Eastern Europe terrorized and gagged, to react." But all things considered, he concluded, "I accept the risk of staying with de Gaulle. Provided, naturally, that he doesn't play the dictator."

It is striking that Mauriac, Malraux, and de Gaulle himself never seem to have concluded that there was any serious alternative other than de Gaulle or the Communists. The Right was so hopelessly compromised during the Occupation that by a feat of verbal legerdemain it vanished, although to this day it controls 40 to 60 percent of the French electorate, *bon an, mal an*. A large portion, as Mauriac notes, took refuge behind the Cross of Lorraine after the liberation; they are still there.

Except for a few honest neo-Fascists, the rest of the Right blandly changed its generic label to center. This has given rise to an amusing spectacle before opening sessions of new assemblies, when former Pétainists indignantly spurn the benches on the right. (The Gaullists tolerantly occupied an arc from center left to far right, granting an enclave to the "centrists" in the upper middle. The confusion in nomenclature has misled some journalists; the French generally let their parties call themselves what they will, but they find it increasingly difficult to call the present régime Gaullist. It is generally referred to now, accurately enough, as "La Majorité.")

As for the democratic Left, de Gaulle held it in total contempt. The French in 1789 would die for the Republic, he observed, "but nobody would die for the Radicals." He considered the Socialists the "clowns" of his first Cabinet—in fact, called all his ministers "lâches!" (jackals might be a good translation). Bidault complained, "If you could see how he treats us, his ministers!"

History has made academic Mauriac's understandable fear that de Gaulle might become a dictator. He saw himself, quite frankly, as a monarch; he spurned a proposal that he be elected to the Académie Française on the ground that "Louis XIV did not join the Academy, Napoleon did not join the Academy." But he was a monarch in the sense that, to him, Tito, Stalin, and even Roosevelt were monarchs—chiefs of state by force of character and, sometimes, by popular consent. When the contract was broken, he was too proud to rule by force.

History has, alas, also confirmed de Gaulle's judgment on the politicians: the revolving Cabinets of 1946–1958, the Indochinese and Algerian wars, Suez, inflation, strikes, and repression. His own successive "Gaullist" parties

successively betrayed him, in 1952 by joining the game of coalitions to obtain ministries; in the late sixties by sabotaging his plans for profit-sharing and "participation" while putting the brakes on wages and welfare, thus provoking the explosion of May 1968; finally, in 1969–1970, by uniting with the "center" that had just helped send him into retirement—proving Malraux's dictum: "Le Gaullisme sans de Gaulle est idiot!"

But the politicians understood the people better than de Gaulle did. "It is deplorable indeed," Malraux told Mauriac in 1946, "that de Gaulle has crystallized all the forces of the Left against him. All that might not have happened if I'd met him earlier. The great weakness of that great mind is this: never has de Gaulle sat at a workman's table." De Gaulle, the resistant, the self-styled revolutionary, may well have held the bourgeoisie in contempt. (He reminded Malraux that John F. Kennedy had burst out, "Daddy told me businessmen were sons of bitches!") But Malraux ruefully observed to Mauriac, "between a bourgeois and him, there is the bridge of a common vocabulary."

It may be doubted, however, that had de Gaulle met Malraux earlier, things would have ended differently. After all, Malraux sat at de Gaulle's right hand in the Cabinet from 1958 to 1969. ("The presence at my side of this brilliant friend, devotee of lofty destinies, gives me the impression of being protected on that flank"—*Memoires d'Espoir*.) De Gaulle did nothing in that time to modify the distribution of wealth in France, the most lopsided in the industrial world. It was de Gaulle's foreign policy that alarmed the privileged classes, while his domestic policy made it impossible for any significant part of the Left to come to his aid.

Malraux himself was always vividly aware of this. In that dialogue of *Les Chênes*, he reproaches de Gaulle for having slighted the partisans during the war (Malraux was, of course,

164

Colonel Berger of the F.F.I.) and tells him: "The Left Gaullists really hope that sooner or later you would do in the social domain what they no longer expected from the Communists or the Socialists; but they didn't follow you for that." There was, then, something left of the revolutionary Malraux of China and Spain, the prewar hero of French intellectuals. They are bitter now when his name is mentioned, not because he broke with the Communists in 1939, but because he turned to a national ideal they identify with the Right. (A recently published doctoral thesis holds that he always was a romantic, never a Marxist.) They do not forgive him for having led the march of frightened, antirevolutionary Parisians up the Champs-Elysées on May 30, 1968; he said later he had not heard the anti-Semitic chants in the crowd.

To Malraux and de Gaulle, in the twilight at Colombey, the "nihilist" uprising of the students was just one more sign of the decline of the West. A mood of defeat infuses both of these books, Mauriac's and Malraux's. On a similar day in 1946, early in his first exile from power de Gaulle told Mauriac, "I have never gone anywhere but from failure to failure." He ticked them off; his prewar effort to endow France with a motorized army, his effort to persuade the Reynaud Government to move from Bordeaux to Algiers and continue the war, his first effort to bring the colonial army into combat, and so on. The list can be extended to cover the failures of his Fifth Republic: he failed to pry Europe from the hegemony of the two Supergrands; he failed to break the hold of the dollar; he failed to persuade the Americans to get out of Vietnam and the Israelis to hold their fire; having finally obtained the constitution that he thought would end the political "combines" that sapped France's will, he had lived to see a combine of his own former creatures and his enemies in power, burying his dreams of grandeur.

And yet, and yet. . . . The humble thousands stood in silence around the church in Colombey; the kings and statesmen, barred from his burial by de Gaulle's proud will, prayed in Notre Dame; a great throng made its way up the Champs-Elysées in the rain, flowers in hand, and many who had hated him wept. It was far from the pomp of Churchill's funeral or the hysteria of Nasser's. It was marked, instead, by an austere nobility, suggesting the passing of something quite unique from the world.

There are some defeats that are more meaningful than some victories. In *Les Chênes*, de Gaulle (or was it Malraux?) says, "Maurice of Saxony, who never lost a battle, is not in the least equal to Napoleon, who ended in defeat. Victories that are only victories don't go very far." Malraux reminds de Gaulle of his magnetic attraction for the masses of the third world, so palpable to anyone who has ever followed one of his tours. In reply, de Gaulle shrewdly jests that the Spanish world may identify him with another favorite, Don Quixote. (The French, of course, finally preferred Sancho Panza—Pompidou.) Then he adds that his only international rival is Tin-tin, the little hero of a French cowboy comic strip.

"We are the little fellows who don't let the big ones take advantage of them," he explained. "It's not noticed, because of my size."

If, in spite of his failures, de Gaulle goes down in history as one of the giants of our epoch, perhaps that is as good a reason as any. In times when all men of common sense acknowledged that the world was fated to be ruled by superpowers, Hitler Germany at one point, the United States and the Soviet Union at another, he stood like King Canute defying the tides, asserting the right of every nation to decide its destiny—and its power to do it if it has the will. Today, we Americans, reviewing the results of a contrary policy, may wish he had been more successful.

165